A Daybook for November

In Yellow Springs, Ohio

A Memoir in Nature

and a Handbook for the Month of November,
Being a Personal Narrative and Synthesis of
Common Events in Nature
between 1981 and 2023
in Southwestern Ohio, with Applications
for the Lower Midwest and Middle Atlantic
Region, Containing Weather Guidelines
and a Variety of Natural Calendars,
Reflections by the Author
and Seasonal Quotations
from Ancient and Modern Writers

By

Bill Felker

A Daybook for the Year in Yellow Springs, Ohio
Volume 11: November

Cover Image from a Watercolor by Libby Rudolf

Copyright 2023 by Bill Felker

Published by The Green Thrush Press
P.O. Box 431, Yellow Springs, Ohio

Printed in the United States of America
Charleston, SC

ISBN: 9781719953030

For Max and Jack

For Max and Jack

No one suspects the days to be gods.

Ralph Waldo Emerson

Introduction

All my botanical walks, the varied impressions made by the places where I have seen memorable things, the ideas they have aroused in me, all this has left me with impressions which are revived by the sight of the plants I have collected in those places....

Jean-Jacques Rousseau, *Reveries of the Solitary Walker*

The Daybook Format

The format of my notes in this daybook owes more than a little to the almanacs I wrote for the *Yellow Springs News* between 1984 and 2017. The quotations, daily statistics, the weather outlooks, the seasonal calendar, and the daybook journal were and still are part of my regular routine of collecting and organizing impressions about the place in which I live.

Setting: The principal habitat described here is that of Glen Helen, a preserve of woods and glades that lies on the eastern border of the village of Yellow Springs in southwestern Ohio. At its northern edge, the Glen joins with John Bryan State Park to form a corridor about ten miles long, and half a mile wide, along the Little Miami River. The north section of the Glen Helen /John Bryan complex is hilly and heavily wooded, and is the best location for spring wildflowers. The southern portion, "South Glen" as it is usually called, is a combination of open fields, wetlands, and wooded flatlands. Here I found many flowers and grasses of summer and fall. Together, the two Glens and John Bryan Park provide a remarkable cross section of the fauna and flora of the eastern United States.

Other habitats in the daybook journal include my yard with its several small gardens; the village of Yellow Springs itself, a town of 4,000 at the far eastern border of the Dayton suburbs; the Caesar Creek Reservoir, twenty miles south of Yellow Springs and created by the Corps of Engineers in 1976. My trips away from that environment were principally northeast to Chicago, Madison, Wisconsin and northern Minnesota, east to Washington and New York, southeast to the Carolinas and Florida, southwest to

Arkansas, Louisiana, and Texas, and occasionally through the Southwest to California and the Northwest, two excursions to Belize in Central America, several to Italy.

Quotations: The passages from ancient and modern writers (and sometimes from my alter egos) which accompany each day's notations are lessons from my readings, as well as from distant seminary and university training, here put to work in service of the reconstruction of my sense of time and space. They are a collection of reminders, hopes, and promises for me that I find implicit in the seasons. They have also become a kind of a cosmological scrapbook for me, as well as the philosophical underpinning of this narrative.

Astronomical Data: The *Daybook* includes approximate dates for astronomical events, such as star positions, meteor showers, solstice, equinox, perihelion (the Sun's position closest to earth), and aphelion (the Sun's position farthest from Earth).

I have included the sunrise and sunset for Yellow Springs as a general guide to the progression of the year in this location, but those statistics also reflect trends that are world wide, if more rapid in some places and slower in others. All times mentioned in the Daybook are given in Eastern Standard Time.

Even though the day's length is almost never exactly the same from one town to the next, a minute gained or lost in Yellow Springs is often a minute lost or gained elsewhere, and the Yellow Springs numbers can be used as a simple way of watching the lengthening or shortening of the days, and, therefore, of watching the turn of the planet. For those who wish to keep track of the Sun themselves in their own location, abundant sources are now available for this information in local and national media.

Average Temperatures: Average temperatures in Yellow Springs are also part of each day's entry. Since the rise and fall of temperatures in other parts of the North America, even though they may start from colder or warmer readings, keep pace with the temperatures here, the highs and lows in Yellow Springs are, like solar statistics, helpful indicators of the steady progress of the year throughout most of the states along the 40th Parallel east of the Mississippi.

Weather: My daily, weekly and monthly weather summaries have been distilled from over thirty years of observations. They are descriptions of the local weather history I have kept in order to track the gradual change in temperatures, precipitation and cloud cover through the year I have also used them in order to try to identify particular characteristics of each day. They are not meant to be predictions.

Although my interest in the Yellow Springs microclimate at first seemed too narrow to be of use to those who lived outside the area, I began to modify it to meet the needs of a number of regional and national farm publications for which I started writing in the mid 1980s. And so, while the summaries are based on my records in southwestern Ohio, they can be and have been used, with interpretation and interpolation, throughout the Lower Midwest , the Middle Atlantic States and the East.

The Natural Calendar: In this section, I note the progress of foliage and floral changes, farm and garden practices, migration times for common birds, and peak periods of insect activity. Some of these notes are second hand; I'm a sky watcher, but not an astronomer, and I rely on the government's astronomical data and a few other references for much of my information about the stars and the sun. I am also a complete amateur at bird watching, and most of the migration dates used in the seasonal calendar come from published sources. And even though I keep close track of the farm year, the percentages listed for planting and harvesting are interpretations of averages supplied by the state's weekly crop reports.

Daybook Entries: The journal entries in the daybook section provide the raw material from which I wrote the Natural Calendar digests. The daybook section is a collection of observations made from the window of my car and from my walks in Glen Helen, in parks and wildlife areas within a few miles of my home, and on occasional trips. It is a record that anyone with a few guidebooks could make, and it includes just a small number of the natural markers that anyone might discover.

When I began to take notes about the world around me, I found that there were few descriptions of actual events in nature available for southwestern Ohio. There was no roadmap for the course of the year. My daily observations, as narrow and incomplete as they were, were especially significant to me since I had found no other narrative of the days, no other depiction of what was actually occurring around me. In time, the world came into focus with each particle I named. I saw concretely that time and space were the sum of their parts.

As my notes for each day accumulated, I could see the wide variation of events that occurred from year to year; at the same time, I saw a unity in this syncopation from which I could identify numerous sub-seasons and with which I could understand better the kind of habitat in which I was living and, consequently, myself. When I paged through the journal entries for each day, I was drawn back to the space in which they were made. I browsed and imagined, returned to the journey.

Journal Essays: At the end of many of the daybook entries, I have included brief essays from my almanac column in the *Yellow Springs News*.

Companions: Many friends, acquaintances and family members have contributed their observations to the daybook, and their participation has taught me that my private seasons are also community seasons, and that all of our experiences together help to lay the foundation for a rich, local consciousness of natural history.

The Month of November
November Averages: 1981 through 2021
Normal November Temperature: 42.6

Year	Average
1981	43.6
1982	43.9
1983	43.1
1984	39.6
1985	47.6
1986	40.4
1987	46.6
1988	43.6
1989	41.0
1990	47.1
1991	39.2
1992	42.8
1993	42.5
1994	48.4
1995	36.1
1996	36.3
1997	38.8
1998	45.2
1999.	47.4
2000	40.4
2001	48.6
2002	39.6
2003	46.5
2004	45.0
2005	43.8
2006	44.0
2007	42.6
2008	40.0
2009	46.4
2010	42.8
2011	47.2
2012	40.9
2013	40.2
2014	37.7
2015	47.0
2014	47.2
2017	42.7
2018	38.2
2019	38.8
2020	47.7
2021	41.8
2022	45.4
2023	44.7

November 1
The 305th Day of the Year

Many of the events of the annual cycle recur year after year in a regular order. A year-to-year record of this order is a record of the rates at which solar energy flows to and through living things. They are the arteries of the land. By tracing their responses to the sun, Phenology may eventually shed some light on that ultimate enigma, the land's inner workings.

Aldo Leopold, *A Phenological Record for Sauk and Dane Counties, Wisconsin, 1935-1945 (1947)*

Sunrise/set: 7:04/5:33
Day's Length: 10 hours 29 minutes
Average High/Low: 57/38
Average Temperature: 48
Record High: 79 – 1950 and 2016
Record Low: 20 – 1906

The Daily Weather

Record highs for November are almost always set during the first days of the month, and today the chances of an afternoon in the 70s is 30 percent. Highs in the 60s come 25 percent of the time, in the 50s thirty percent, in the 40s, 30s and 20s five percent each. This is also one of the sunniest days of the month, with a 70 percent chance of clear to partly cloudy skies. Frost occurs on only 15 percent of the mornings, and rain falls half the years.

The Weather in the Week Ahead

The chances of warmth in the 70s drop to just three to five percent on November 4, and odds increase for cold throughout the week ahead. Highs just in the 30s or 40s were relatively rare during the final days of October, but by the 5th of November, they occur 25 percent of the time, and chances rise to over 40 percent by the 10th of the month.

The coolest days in this period are typically the 6th and the 7th, both of which have only about a 15 percent chance of warmth in the 60s. The 3rd ushers in the snow season for this part of the country, flurries or accumulation emerging into the realm of possibility, at least a ten percent possibility per day between that date and spring.

Chances of a thunderstorm virtually disappear until February, but all-day rains increase. The first ten days of November are about twice as rainy as the final ten of October. Chances of rain or snow run at about 40 percent from the 1st through the 5th, then drop to just 15 to 20 percent on the 6th, 7th, and 8th.

The November Outlook

November's average temperatures fall one degree every 50 hours, finding the middle 30s by the end of the month. Normal highs slip down to the middle 40s and lows dip below 30 by December 1st. With averages plummeting about 14 degrees, around 15 mornings below freezing occur in the next 30 days at average elevations along the 40th Parallel.

There is an average of only one or two days in the 70s, just six in the 60s and only eight in the 50s. That makes just half the month with moderate afternoons, and many of those fall within a week of All Saints Day (November 1st). The coldest days in November, those with better than a 35 percent chance of a high below 40 degrees, are the 12th, 13th, 15th, 18th, 21st, 24th, 28th, 29th, and 30th. The days with the best chances of highs in the 60s and 70s are usually the 1st through the 4th.

In the entire month of November, five to six completely clear days can be expected, ten or eleven partly cloudy days, and about 13 mostly or completely cloudy ones. Odds are even that most of the warmer days will be cloudy. The sky becomes especially gray after the 14th of the month, the solar pivot time when the Midwest darkens until May, and the percentage of sunshine in an average day drops from 60 percent to 40 percent.

Overcast skies are likely to bring rain 11 out of the next 30 days. Snow or sleet is ordinarily recorded on between one and four occasions before December 1st, the first snow almost always arriving between the 10th and the 20th.

The darkest November days, those with just a 15 to 30 percent chance of sun, are the 15th, the 23rd, and the 28th. The rainiest periods of the month are usually between the 1st and the 5th, the 9th and the 11th, the 15th and the 17th, the 25th through the 29th, each carrying at least a 35 percent chance of precipitation. Of those days, the 5th, 9th, 15th, 20th, 23rd, 26th, and especially the 27th are the wettest of all. Odds for snow are best on the 28th, 29th, and 30th. The driest days for harvest are typically the 8th, the 13th, the 18th, and the 21st, each with only a 15 percent chance of rain or snow.

Autumncount

Eighteen major weather systems cross the United States in an average autumn. Four of those fronts arrived in September, six in October. Seven additional cold waves, most of them accompanied by precipitation, cross the Mississippi in the next 30 days (the final Autumncount front coming on December 3rd). Mild conditions are common until the first weather system arrives.

November 2: As November arrives, frost often moves into the Border States, and the odds increase for cold throughout the week ahead. The 3rd ushers in the snow season for the nation's midsection, flurries or accumulation becoming at least a ten percent possibility per day between that date and spring. Chances of a thunderstorm usually disappear until February in the Midwest, but all-day rains increase. If this first November front is a day or two late, the 1st through the 3rd or 4th can be some of the mildest days of late autumn.

November 6: This weather system usually brings the coldest days of November's first week. It also carries Middle Fall into the Border States and the South, Late Fall to the Midwest and southern Plains, and Early Winter to farms along the Canadian border. The days immediately after the November 6th front are usually much more moderate, but precipitation is the rule as the next system approaches. Beginning at this time of month, the percentage of daily sunlight drops quickly, and the wind blows a little harder, rising to its winter levels.

November 11: Sun often follows this front, and the 11th, 12th and 13th are often some of the best days in the first half of the month for harvest. A dramatic increase in the number of freezing predawn temperatures starts with this system, the lows below 32 growing from a frequency average of 40 percent up to 70 percent across the nation's midsection.

November 16: As this front approaches, expect milder conditions, but an increased chance of rain or snow. Although the November 16th system can be relatively gentle, sometimes it brings highs only in the teens or even 20s as far south as Kentucky. After the front moves through, favorable harvest conditions typically follow: the 18th is one of the drier November days in the Midwest, the 17th in the Plains, the 19th in the East.

November 20: The cycle of the November 20th weather system causes milder conditions before its arrival and increased chances of precipitation. This is a front that carries up to two or more inches of snow across the North four years in a decade. After the system comes through, it can be followed by single digits in the North, and a hard freeze deep into the South.

November 24: This sixth cold front of the month, arriving around the 24th, often brings rain or significant snowfall as it passes through. After the 25th, the percentage of cloudy days almost doubles over the average for the rest of November; even in the South, overcast conditions begin to increase the likelihood for seasonal affective disorders and contribute to complications with harvest. This weather system marks the decline of average highs below 50 degrees and the end to any reasonable chance of a day above 70 throughout the Midwest and Mid-Atlantic states. Average low temperatures fall below freezing throughout the North. As the final weather system of the month approaches, however, the 26th is sometimes one of the windiest and mildest days in late November.

November 28: The seventh high-pressure system of November generally arrives around the 28th, preceded by rain or snow three years out of four. This is one of the most dangerous weather systems of the month, and precipitation lingers through the cold for the 29th and 30th. Clouds dominate the sky, and travel conditions are typically uncertain. The weather ordinarily moderates around the last day of November, setting the stage for an early December thaw.

Barometric Contours of Autumn

The temporal countryside takes on its autumnal contours from the increasingly violent movements of the Earth's atmosphere as it tilts away from the sun.

Graphs of barometric pressure reveal many of the topographical patterns of the season. August's barometric configurations are slow and gentle like low, rolling dunes. Heat waves show up as wide plateaus. Thunderstorms are sharp, shallow troughs in the mellow waves of the atmospheric landscape.

At the close of Late Summer, the year has begun its ascent to the steep cliffs of December. By the beginning of October, the barometric waves are stronger; the high-pressure peaks become taller; the lows are deeper, with almost every valley bringing rain.

Tapering floral sequences and the gradual surge of leafturn occur amid the diminishing prairie of middle September. From the broad lowland of warmth with its six months of birdsong and its hundred days of insect calls, the sun pulls the land up into the foothills of the year where asters and goldenrod bloom and where trees are gold and red.

Middle Fall is the rough piedmont of another country, stripping foliage, putting buds into dormancy, burning away the undergrowth and revealing the dark hillsides. At the end of Late Fall, December's great range of cold and snow fills the horizon. Beyond it lies another immense upland, the frigid, high plateau of Deep Winter in which nothing ever seems to grow or change until the ground crumbles and gives way, shattered by thaws, and time tumbles down into the sudden, stormy gorge of March.

Frostwatch

The following chart shows the chances that frost will often have occurred by the date indicated. Calculations are based on typical frequency of freezing temperatures at average elevations along the 40th Parallel during the month of October. The data can be adjusted roughly by adding five percent for each 100 miles north or south that Parallel. Local frost histories, of course, offer much greater detail.

Date	Chance of Light Frost	Chance of Killing Frost
November 1:	99 percent	80 percent
November 10:		90 percent
November 20:		95 percent
November 25:		99 percent

Key to the Nation's Weather

The typical November temperature, the average of the high of 50 and the low of 35, at median elevations along the 40th Parallel is 42 degrees. Using the following chart based on weather statistics from around the country, one can calculate the approximate temperatures in other locations. For example, with the average of the 40th Parallel as the base of "42," you can estimate normal temperatures in Portland, Maine by subtracting four degrees from 42 degrees. Or add 20 degrees to find out the likely average (42 + 20 = 62 degrees) in New Orleans during the month.

Fairbanks, Alaska	-38
Minneapolis	-9
Portland, Maine	-4
Detroit	-3
Des Moines	-3
Chicago	-2
AVERAGE ALONG 40TH PARALLEL	42
Seattle	+4
St. Louis	+4
Washington, D.C.	+4
Las Vegas	+11
Dallas	+12
Charleston, SC	+17
Los Angeles	+19
New Orleans	+20
Miami, FL	+30

November Phenology

When all the mums are past their best, then major bird migrations will soon be over for the year.

When the yellow witch hazel blooms, gardeners should put in spring bulbs and dormant roses, and mulch perennials. Farmers should plant the final winter wheat and complete the harvest of corn of soybeans

When thimbleweed heads are tufted like cotton, then Late Fall arrives with killing frosts. That's the time to market goat and sheep cheese, Christmas cacti, dried flowers and grasses, poinsettias, mistletoe and ginseng for the holidays.

When Christmas cacti start to bud, then climbing bittersweet opens in the woods and almost every junco has arrived for winter.

The budding of Christmas cacti is also a marker for planting amaryllis and paperwhite bulbs for mid-December blooms.

When autumn violets end their season beside the woodland paths, then strawberries can be mulched with straw and peonies divided and transplanted.

When the last maple leaves fall, test the field and garden soil, and mow the lawn for the last time. Dig manure into the garden. Plant next year's sweet peas and spinach. Set garlic cloves for spring.

When all the leaves are down, then fertilize trees and shrubs and remove tops from everbearing raspberries.

As mock orange and forsythia foliage thins, it measures the advance of winter. When all their leaves are down, a killing frost has occurred even in the mildest autumns.

When deer rutting season reaches its peak, then pastures are normally dormant. Only in subtropical Florida do Bermuda and Johnson grass, chenopods and amaranths continue to bloom.

When the poinsettia crop arrives at the market, then the last crickets die in the cold and many farmers are feeding hay to their livestock.

When beech and pear leaves finally fall, then wrap young transplants to protect them against frost cracking.

Natural Calendar

The transition time to Late Fall brings the close of Mum Season, Autumn Violet Season, Aster Season, Goldenrod Season and Katydid Season. Korean Lilac Leafdrop Season ends in the garden. White Mulberry Leafturn Season and Ginkgo Leafturn Season brighten the canopy for a few days, and then the foliage of those trees often shatters overnight. In the greenhouse, Jade Tree Flowering Season complements the gathering tide of Christmas Cactus Flowering Season.

The Stars

As November begins, the Summer Triangle is setting in the west , and Orion is coming up in the east, the Milky Way tying them together through the Great Square. By the arrival of Deep Winter, Orion will be almost overhead at bedtime, and Gemini will tower behind it.

The evenings of Early Spring push Orion deep into the west, bring Cancer and Leo overhead, and by the time Late Spring reaches the 40th Parallel, Orion will have disappeared from the dark sky, and boxy Libra will be rising in the southeast, the Corona Borealis above it.

In Early Summer, the Summer Triangle returns to evening in the east, forecasting the Dog Days of July . When its constellations of Lyra, Cygnus and Aquiila are directly above you, the trees will be their deepest green and the autumn migrations will be underway. And just as the leaves come down, Orion will be up again at the beginning of the night, retelling the time of year.

Daybook

1982: Most of the maple leaves in town fell overnight in the wind and rain. The cherry leaves are down in the backyard. Catalpas long gone. Many ginkgoes still have full foliage, deep gold and losing leaves slowly.

1983: Ginkgoes turning quickly now at my window and on Herman Street and Xenia Avenue. The maples in front of the house have lost two thirds of their leaves.

1985: Cherry leaves in the yard are all still green, cherry the most unpredictable and capricious of our autumn trees.

1986: Along King Street, a few chicory, thyme-leafed speedwell, and Queen Anne's lace are still flowering; Osage all full yellow green, dogwoods yellow, green, and pink. There are still violets blooming. The pond at the end of Cemetery Street is full of geese.

1987: South Glen, 75 degrees. Cabbage butterflies still common. Wood ducks migrating down river, blackbirds clucking, kingfishers screaming and racing back and forth above the water. Some robins in the honeysuckles. A large flock of doves by the second fishing hole (one carp caught 11:15 a.m.). The canopy is gone, but the path is still green, dappled with late violets. Ironweed is white for picking, and goldenrod and thimbleweed are pale and bushy like thistledown throughout the undergrowth. Barberries, rose hips, and coralberry shine in the dull fields and hedgerows. The very last asters are in bloom. Grasshoppers still here, crickets loud. With all the trees and shrubs bare, the river reflects the whole blue sky against the last golden leaves along the bank. In town, Bradford pears are deep, rich red. Most Osage gone (those with fruits), while those without are golden. One Osage variety seems immune to frost; the other blackens at the first hard freeze.

1988: Flocks of starlings and geese are flying over almost every day. All ginkgo leaves gone. Lil's maple 80 percent gone. Oaks still red and brown, full color. My sweet gum tree keeps half its foliage. Cherry and pussy willow still keep most of their leaves. Most maple raking for the year is done, garden full of mulch.

1989: Geese fly over 8:39 a.m. My ginkgo is a third gone.

1990: My ginkgo is full gold today, the complete transformation accomplished since October 29th. Along the way into Yellow Springs on Grinnell, the canopy above the road is gone. A brown ridge of branches, highlighted by red and orange oaks, remains above the valley. My poplar at home thins quickly, maybe a third left. Mums still strong and bright.

1992: The quince falls quickly now, leaves yellow and speckled. Last phase of leaf color beginning: most maples gone, oaks still full, accentuated by scattered remnants. Grass bright green in the rain. The mums in the south garden are lanky but are still at full color; snapdragon foliage holds, a few small-flowered yarrow cut, foliage fresh. Two strawberries lie red in the garden, sweet and firm.

1997: The leaves continue to hold in this latest of possible autumns. Even the maple in front of our house, usually the first to go at the end of the third week in October, has half its leaves, all golden. Around town, the maples are still at their peak, joined now with the red sweet gums and the golden and maroon oaks. Maggie says that the leaves are holding in Madison, Wisconsin, too, that last week there was a snow that held so beautifully to the late foliage.

1998: A few crows at 6:34 a.m. Then a little later, several hundred crows swooped into town and sat in some bare maples on Limestone Street. In the greenhouse today, I found that a caterpillar had eaten most of one of my tomato plants, left his droppings on a leaf and disappeared.

1999: Lil's maple starting to lose leaves now. Danielson's almost done. Barberries, pears, and burning bush full and bright red throughout the village. This afternoon, a white cabbage moth flew by the yellow heart-shaped leaves of the redbud tree.

2003: One cardinal sang at 6:50 this morning. Another cardinal song at 7:20. By 7:30, blackbirds had started their clucking in the back trees. A large flock of blackbirds seen cleaning up a soybean field on the way to Dayton. In the greenhouse, Christmas cacti, red, white, violet, are in full bloom. In the south garden, almost all the Korean lilac leaves have fallen, had turned a deep yellow before they fell. The pink quince foliage is thin, but golden. One of the red mulberry trees along the south border has lost about two thirds of its leaves; the other still has most of its leaves.

2004: The magnolia across the street is almost bare. The pink quince bush has lost about three-fourths of its leaves. Red mulberry trees are losing leaves, are down to half. The white mulberry is turning all at once. Many dogwoods are a rich, deep red throughout town. In the countryside, only the yellow Osage foliage stands out. In the south garden, the soil temperature is 57.

2005: Out in the countryside, leafturn has passed the peak, but full gold remains in many woodlots. I estimate that maybe half of the trees are down. Along High Street, Lil's and Mrs. Timberlake's maples are still full, Danielson's about a fourth gone. At Wilberforce, all the ashes and most of the locusts have fallen. One ginkgo is two-thirds shed, the others still green.

2006: Leafturn is way past its best now along the road to Wilmington. Lil's tree half down, Timberlake's almost all down. A small flock of robins in the alley this morning at 8:30. A cardinal was singing when I went outside at 6:40. I've finished putting ten yards of mulch around the yard, have cut the grass and mulched some of the leaves into the lawn. The garden is clearly outlined now, neat and ordered for winter and spring, as beautiful as I've ever seen it. The quince is full gold. Walking with Bella, I imagined the power of the "thin time," the space between seasons, the communion of the living and the dead, the call of second spring, the call of winter's rest.

2007: A cardinal sang while I walked Bella in the dark alley this morning at 6:40. A wren was chattering in the back yard when we got home. Mild weather continues, with frost in the mornings, clear sky, Venus so bright. The oaks are turning now in the Mills Lawn Park.

2009: To Yellow Springs from Fancy Gap, Virginia, full sun, temperatures in the 50s by afternoon: Throughout the mountains of Virginia, West Virginia and Ohio, Late Fall has arrived, with oaks, some maples and sweet gums offering variety and color to the hills. A few asters seen and sundrops yesterday in the Carolinas. But the news is late autumn above Statesville, NC, all the way to Yellow Springs. Road kills – many young raccoons and opossums, many deer. Only one flock of starlings in the whole 1,500 miles of our trip this past week.

2010: Frost finally wilted the elephant ears last night. More sun and dry today. Sweet gums stay full yellow and bright red. Tree line foliage in town is motley and broken.

2011: Zelkova trees full maroon, Lil's maple bright gold and shedding, Mrs. Timberlake's paler and with fewer leaves. Many oaks gone in the park, deep orange and red-orange maples taking their place. Stonecrop added to the front garden, three blackberry bushes to the raised beds. Sweet gum thinning to half. A blue jay fed all day at the back feeder. One sulfur butterfly seen as I drove along the highway north.

2013: In the Phillips Street alley, the canopy opens further as the tree of heaven branches come down. I found the first red winterberry and the first red-orange bittersweet berries pushing out from their blushing hulls. Handfuls of starlings in the bare high branches, robins whinnying west of High Street. Frank's silver maple with pale shading. The Dayton-Street beech is gilded this morning. The post office Zelcova is deep orange and red-orange. On the way to Jamestown, a small murder of crows feeding on road kill. At Ellis Pond, all the oaks except for the sawtooth oak have suddenly turned brown or red-brown, following the lead of Lil's maple of several days ago. Several sycamores and tulip trees are mostly bare. Half the sugar maples on the south side of the water have come down; all the bald cypresses have turned, and their brittle needles lie in clumps across the long grass. A few white asters still blooming by the shore.

2014: First flurries this morning, gusty wind, and the white mulberry leaves have started to come down.

2015: Several crickets with long trilling calls were active until about 6:30 this morning. A cardinal sang at 6:50, answered by another far away. Crows came by a little after 7:00. A red-tailed hawk flew crying overhead while I did tai chi on the back porch. I cleared the zinnias and the last tithonias from the north garden, planted the remainder of the daffodils (70 in all) in the circle garden and Jeanie's redbud garden. When I finished about 10:00, the first grackle I've heard or seen in a long time was clucking in the white mulberry tree. And robins were peeping steadily in the honeysuckles all through the morning. Now the Norway maple in Jerry and Lee's yard, planted relatively recently maybe by

Jimmie's mother, and another Norway in Don's back yard are rivaling Lil's maple for the latest on the block to shed.

2016: Sun and near-record high of 79 this afternoon. In the zinnias, a common buckeye (*Junonia coenia*), a cabbage white, a pale sulphur, small bumblebees and honeybees. Mrs. Timberlake's maple is full and shedding, the Danielsons' bare, Don's two sugar maples anchoring the corner of High and Dayton Streets with dense orange. High leaf color holds throughout the village. The hops are dark and withered, and the grape vines are all pale, winding through the honeysuckles. The maple grove at Ellis Pond is a rich and variegated rusty brown. The tulipo and the dogwoods are deep purple-scarlet, the red maples veined with gold and pink, some silver maples turning palomino. On the way to the Catholic graveyard, near the wetland area, I saw two more sulphurs and four more cabbage whites, an azure, and what appeared to be a hackberry butterfly (*Asterocampa celtis*). At about 3:15 p.m., a long flock of grackles flew across the north end of the village, traveling northeast to southwest. Vibrant chorus of katydids and crickets this mild evening in the high 60s.

2017: Before flying into the Midwest and cold and steady rain, I walked with Jeni in Portland: Cool and sunny, the sweet gum trees deep red and starting to come down.

2018: A stormy All Saints' Day, peak leaf color holding throughout town, even as the early maples came down in yesterday's wind. Moya's maple collapsed overnight, but the bright Dayton Street maples now shine through even stronger. In the greenhouse, the large Christmas cacti have small buds.

2019: The first low in the 20s (27) this morning.

2020: Hard winds with rising barometer and dropping temperatures throughout the day, full moon a day old. At Pearl's Fen, almost all the canopy is empty, chinquapin oak leaves, maples and sycamores covering the paths. Goldenrod flowers have become gray seed tufts. In the afternoon, the first snow showers crossed the area, and when we drove to Xenia we saw that the ginkgo at the corner of

Marshall and Xenia Avenue had collapsed. Lil's tree has thinned to maybe half, and Mrs. Timberlake's has joined the Danielsons' bare maple.

2022: Geese flew over this morning before 8:00, the day soft and tattered from yesterday's rain. Lil's burning bush foliage has dropped.

2023: First light snow in then night, the morning clear and crisp.

Journal

O angels, blessed in numbers vast,
Protect and guard us on life's way
Against all evils of the past,
Those yet to come, those of this day.

From *Christe, redemptor, omnium*, Vigils Hymn for All Saints Day, November 1, in the Ancient Christian Office of the Hours

I grew up surrounded by icons and rosaries and holy practices. Now at the turning of the season, when all the leaves come down and I lose the security and warmth of summer, I am especially aware of my vulnerability, and of the mystery, both for better and for worse, of my belief in spirits.

In times of personal or social stress, I do not forget the guardian angel to whom I always prayed. I used to imagine him on my right side, balancing the bad angel on my left side. I still feel him as a presence, when I think of him at all, still there.

What effect could he have now? Is he superstition purely? Is he a seasonal ghost of the Thin Time between fall and winter, between my childhood and my old age? Or is he real power, a relentless energy, to be conjured through my fear by my will? What could he possibly do for me? What cultural-religious baggage does he slyly carry for me? Do I dismiss him at my peril?

A hymn for the Christian feast of All Saints Day (November 1) invokes all spirit creatures, angels and souls of those who have gone before us, to come to our assistance, asserting that we are not alone, that there is continuity between the living and the dead, strength in their coexistence. This is a time of chill and danger, the tradition says, time to invoke and hold close the allies.

Ah, see! among the newly leafless trees,
the first new leaf: the moon!
under the owl's dark wing,
as winter coming,
the one unfurled leaf
among dark boughs, dark boles
where in sheathed buds
lurks, waiting secretly, the spring.

August Derleth

Sunrise/set: 7:05/5:32
Day's Length: 10 hours 27 minutes
Average High/Low: 57/38
Average Temperature: 47
Record High: 77 – 1961 and 2016
Record Low: 20 – 1954

The Daily Weather

Rain falls 35 percent of the time, light snow five percent, on this date. Highs in the 70s occur 10 percent of the afternoons. Sixties are recorded on 25 percent of the years, 50s on 30 percent, 40s on 25 percent, 30s on five percent, and 20s on five percent. Frost strikes one night in five, and the sun appears on 55 percent of the days.

The Natural Calendar

The workday begins to shrink more quickly now, losing about two minutes every 24 hours: November takes almost an hour from the day's length along the 40th Parallel. All the major migrations (except for the migration of gulls and sandhill cranes) end within the next two weeks. Throughout the month, bulbs, shrubs, and dormant roses can still be set out, but November's first week usually provides the most pleasant weather for outdoor activities.

By this stage of the autumn, soil temperatures often fall

into the middle 40s, and the grazing season ends in most Midwestern pastures. Pond waters are at or below 50 degrees, and koi are reluctant to rise for their food. Sugar beets are typically more than three-fourths dug, and the pumpkin harvest nears completion. Orchids reach full bloom in conservatories throughout the country.

Daybook

1982: South Glen woods: Canopy gone. All the flowers have died back, but foliage is bright on violets, garlic mustard, waterleaf, henbit, celandine, smooth-leafed dock, cinquefoil, sweet rocket, yarrow. Small flock of doves in the sycamores. A few crickets heard tonight.

1983: Lil's maple turned overnight. Our maples and Mrs. Lawson's lost their leaves today (two days later than last year) Ginkgoes solid gold outside my window at school.

1985: In the chilly, rainy afternoon, craneflies the size of mosquitoes spin near the front porch. Our pie cherry tree is just starting to turn. Lil's maple almost full yellow. Tree of heaven has lost most of its branches. The Osage is speckled, yellow, holding maybe two thirds of its leaves. Doves noticed in the back woods behind the house.

1986: Cardinal sings at 6:55 a.m., a few minutes before sunrise. The river nude, with new curves, its lizard's tail all withered. Migrating robins heard up the hill. One carp caught at the far fishing hole, 11:55 a.m. Lil's maple three-fourths gone. Ginkgo by my window finally starting to turn.

1987: Cincinnati, 77 degrees: Chicory blooming strong by the roadsides. In Dayton, the tree line is shining yellow as though this were a warm April day and a giant hedge of forsythia were blossoming.

1990: Crickets remain loud day and night. Flies are out in the sun. At the mill, all the colors are crisp against the blue sky; and the newly emerged backdrop of brown earth and leaves makes the remaining greens stand out. Across the street, Lil's maple is full gold and falling.

1991: Uncle Bill called from Gentilly, Minnesota, a blizzard there today. Here in Yellow Springs almost a thousand miles south: flurries.

1994: Robins are still all over the Glen, socializing, feasting on berries, bathing in the river, swooping back and forth; they seem to be celebrating, planning, courting. Turkey vultures still circle above Grinnell Road.

1995: The sugar maple in front of the house finally dropped the rest of its leaves today. Most of the maples held on an extra week this year.

1996: The days overlap from year to year, and in their repetitions are their subtle movements showing only sometimes in my observations, and lost until I look again and find my moments reappearing like black and wet November ginkgoes through the morning fog.

1999: Cloudy, windy, cold and rainy, sleet in the rain, leaves collapsing: the Late Fall cold front is again on time. The ginkgoes in Oakwood are all solid gold, half down around their trunks. Utter beauty of the unraveling landscape, disheveled elegance, decadent display of such color, such patterns.

2000: Two thirds of the sweet gum leaves are down, almost all the maples. Sulphurs, yellow butterflies with black edges on their wings, are mating in the field behind my pine trees.

2001: Yesterday I saw buzzards over the bike path heading south. Only a few scattered wildflowers left here, a couple of tall bellflowers, some small coneflowers, two asters. Goldenrod has lost all its foliage. At the library, oakleaf hydrangea leaves are purple. Hawthorn leaves are red. Sweet gums thinning quickly.

2002: I watched the late fourth-quarter moon rising about an hour before dawn, its tips pointing up like horns, the dark lunar shadow clear in the transparent sky. In the yard, a killing frost. Late morning: a flock of grackles in the back trees. A few robins eating honeysuckle berries at noon. Along the freeway, the first tier of leaves is finally down. The other tiers are holding on a week to ten days past their average drop date.

2003: A cardinal sang at 6:45 this morning. I went outside at 7:10 in the soft 60-degree morning. The starlings were already in full song, their volume increasing in the 20 minutes I sat in the yard. I heard crows, blue jays and a wren. Squirrels played in the bare black walnut trees, hung upside down eating nuts. Lil's maple is shedding quickly, as is Lee and Jerry's, more than half down. Mrs. Timberlake's maple is well ahead of Lil's, several days behind the Danielsons' (which is already bare). As I worked outside in the warm afternoon, I saw three or four cabbage butterflies, several wasps, a yellow sulphur and a new painted lady (*Cynthia*), her colors deep and bright. Nestled in a late-blooming purple coneflower, two bumblebees, one small.

2004: The star magnolia is down, the pink quince almost gone. The three oaks by the church park have lost most of their leaves. Whistling crickets still whistle through the mild, damp nights.

2005: Asian lady beetles continue to fly around the house. Lil's maple still a rich gold, the burning bush deep red below it. The Danielsons' maple maybe a third down, Mrs. Timberlake's matching Lil's. The magnolia down the street has hardly started. Lee and Jerry's sweet gum is still solid green. Oaks are brown and red by the church. Redbuds falling quickly. Grape leaves come down from the vine in the ash at the southeast corner of the yard.

2006: After a freeze in the upper 20s this morning, almost all of the white mulberry leaves came down in the back yard. All the Yellow Springs ginkgoes along Dayton Street fell overnight, and at Wilberforce, all of my ginkgo trees were bare and the red maples in the parking lot were more than half down. As I drove to Wilmington, I watched heavy leafdrop from sugar maples throughout the area. At home, most of the maples are finished along High Street, magnolias losing leaves, wisteria leaves gone. Sweet gums are full color along the highway and at Jerry and Lee's house, half shed in other locations. Mateo's foliage of elm and red mulberry has disappeared. The peak is long gone everywhere.

2009: Yellow Springs – after almost a week in the South: The Dayton Street beech tree is half down. Lil's maple, the secret maple, the Danielsons' and Mrs. Timberlake's are gone. The white mulberry is full yellow, the Osage mostly yellow, redbuds full turn, and the red one by the stump is mostly gone. Dusky purple leaves on the oakleaf hydrangea. Orange berries fully emerged on the bittersweet, pale hulls on the sidewalk. Many honeysuckle bushes almost bare. Anna Belle hydrangea leaves pale, leaves gone from variegated Japanese knotweed. Lilacs mostly gone, quince leaves fill the pond, gold through the water. Gooseneck foliage red and cream and rust, hobblebush paling. Tufted false boneset, some tufts on the New England asters, Peggy's virgin's bower about done, lush long comfrey. Late phlox and the Knockout roses keep showing color. Only red hips on Don's multiflora rosebush.

2010: Buzzards seen over the Glen today.

2011: A mild and sunny day, some high sweeping cirrus clouds, many contrails. Crows were up early in the mild dawn, calling at 6:45, and I saw the cardinal pair at the feeder in the morning twilight. Two buzzards overhead, and Ruby sent a note with a photo of the kettle of buzzards she saw last week. There were dozens more, she said, clustering at their roost at Corry and President Street. Along Xenia Avenue, the ginkgoes are all gold, but their leaves are holding. Dogwood trees all over town are deep red. One cabbage white butterfly seen this afternoon while I was planting daffodils and tulips along the north garden fence. Tonight, the temperature dropping into the middle 50s, I heard scattered intermittent "lisping" crickets and at least three loud katydids between the park and Gerard's.

2013: Yesterday's winds and rain brought down the last red viburnum leaves at the north side of the house, and the south hackberry tree is now bare (the north hackberry holding at about a third).

2014: The first hard frost of the fall. The morning still and crisp. The white mulberry leaves clatter down, all green, covering the back lawn. Lil's maple is down. The red leaves of the viburnum by the side of the house are gone. The great castor bean plants, two of them maybe ten-feet tall, are blackened and broken. In the neighborhood, showers of leaves throughout my walk. Robins peeping, starlings chattering, crows and a hawk in the distance. Moya who lives next door said she has been getting raspberries throughout October and even some this morning, the latest she's ever had them. At Ellis Pond this afternoon, wind warm, a golden sulphur butterfly. In downtown Yellow Springs, the city cut down the row of Bradford pears that lined the main street, ending decades of the markers provided by their April blossoms and their December leaf-fall.

2015: Bright, warm day, one cabbage white, zigzag goldenrod flowers all tufted.

2016: A cardinal sang as I walked Jill down Limestone Street at 6:45 this morning, crows following a few minutes later, sky rose and violet and gold before dawn. Only a few honeybees and small bumblebees today in the zinnias. One cabbage white seen as I drove to the post office. Now Lil's maple is completely yellow-gold, paced well by Mrs. Timberlake's and Don's. All the burning bushes on the block are solid red. Peak color still holds in the village, but the woodlots are bare except for oaks and maples. At the bird feeders, a day with chickadees, sparrows, red-bellied woodpeckers, tufted titmice, cardinals. Janet's redbud has lost its leaves, but the other redbuds keep most of theirs. In the honeysuckle hedge, the climbing bittersweet berries glow like brass.

2017: I have been bringing together all my almanac notes for the past thirty years. I try to separate myself from my observations, but that is becoming more difficult. It is becoming clearer to me that these notes are autobiographical, even though they seem to have little to do with me and everything to do with the trivia of what is happening at certain times throughout the small world in which I live.

Events that supposedly take place outside me are actually internal events. If external reality, as Einstein asserted, is altered by observation, how much more is the observer's reality altered by observing and by the internalizing of external events.

Anyone who stays in a house or town or relationship for an extended period of time undergoes this change. Since both observer and observed, subject and object, are completely porous, association, over time, permeates body and spirit. Certain pieces of land or a garden or furniture take on lives of their own inside the one who lives with them. They grow into the self and resist exorcism, persist in memory and affect and flesh.

And so the hundreds of thousands of words I have collected in my daybook for the year in Yellow Springs seep into me and out of me, and they are both the walk and the talk. They are not unlike the objects in my house and yard with which I live and which are mnemonic and charged with story. They are not unlike the unwritten pieces of my life that shape my consciousness and unconsciousness, except that they are words that have shape and take up space in black and white.

2018: The Zelcovas in front of the post office are full rusty gold today, the decorative elms along Xenia Avenue pale gold and shedding at the top.

2018: To Cincinnati: full late color holds throughout, with the rich reds of pears, sweet gums and oaks beside the remaining maples.

2020: First hard frost in the night, the castor beans melting, white mulberry leaves falling.

2021: Two light frosts so far, a low in the 20s forecast for the next three nights, fruit of new moon and perigee. The village reached peak leaf color on Halloween and remains vibrant and varied up and down the streets. Lil's maple is now all gold and orange, the Daniesons' completely bare, Mrs. Timberlake's holding but thin, the secret maple behind my property gilded in the setting sun. I continue to plant tulips (80 so far) and dig cannas. Talked to Peter today; he said that, for the first summer in years, he had seen no praying mantises.

2022: Morning robins peeping. No starlings since spring, the autumn starlings no longer appearing. Ginkgoes half down, Lil's maple mostly fallen, the maples in town mostly bare, many zelcovas and sweet gums still bright, Moya's yellow poplar keeping its leaves. Harvest is almost done, fields gray and dark instead of gold and beige. Geese fly over morning and evening. Indoors, the first flowers of the red Christmas cactus have opened all the way.

2023; This is the edge of the winter, the end of the summer world. Now the evenings are dark. Sunset has reached within just a quarter hour of its solstice time. Peak leaf color is over. The ginkgoes, the sweet gums and white mulberries are falling. The euonymus berries are white, the bittersweet berries browning, the black pokeberries brittle. Remaining leaves shine like flowers, April colors in fragments instead of banks or drifts.

I found a large late autumn crocus that came up in the middle of the night, standing straight and imposing in spite of the threat of frost. I don't remember planting it. It is easy for me, to think of the crocus as the first of the flowers of the new year like the green cornucopia of Second Spring foliage in the Glen: fresh, tall watercress, wide dock, parsnips, sweet rocket, chickweed, sweet Cicely, bushy hemlock. Robins chirp and cluck in the honeysuckles. Walking down Livermore Street on Halloween, Jill and I saw monarch butterfly, heading south past decorations of ghouls and goblins.

The geese started flying back and forth around the village in September, getting ready for feeding in the fields and gathering at Ellis. Through the past decades, they have come together near this place, and I used to think they foretold autumn. The call of geese used to make me restless to be moving on. Their sound was haunting and sad, told me of all the things I could be missing or had lost already because of my domesticity, my reluctance to pack up and fly away.

Now I see they getting ready for spring. Their rituals are seamless. They embody the momentum of the last and the first seasons, transforming the collapse of the canopy into the anticipation of mating.

The other day I counted almost 150 geese floating and playing on the pond. If past years are any indication, at least a hundred or more will join them for the next four months of winter fellowship. Then they will pair up and be off to find nesting sites by early March. I am cheered by their stability and their dependability, their rites of renewal right now, which show both sides of the world's end.

To finish the moment, to find the journey's end in every step of the road, to live the greatest number of good hours, is wisdom. Since our office is with moments, let us husband them. Let us be poised, and wise, and our own, today.

Ralph Waldo Emerson

November 3rd
The 307th Day of the Year

Every year,
accompanied by a change in the weather,
The ginkgo reverses its magnetic field
And drops a sheet of gold at its feet
Like a metronome shedding time,
Like a skeleton shedding cellular richness
To stand like a lightning rod for the sun.

Robert Paschell

Sunrise/set: 7:06/5:31
Day's Length: 10 hours 25 minutes
Average High/Low: 56/38
Average Temperature: 47
Record High: 77 – 1987
Record Low: 13 – 1951

The Daily Weather

Chances of highs in the 70s are 15 percent, for 60s fifteen percent, for 50s twenty-five percent, for 40s forty percent, for 30s five percent. Rain comes four days in a decade, snow one day in a decade. Skies are overcast 40 percent of the time. Morning frosts occur one night out of two.

The Natural Calendar

Indian Summer
lies. I will be deceived by
delinquent crickets.

John Blakelock

Through the last days of Middle Fall, almost half of the forsythia, silver olive, mock orange and honeysuckle foliage holds on. Some years, the pears and silver maples, Osage and white mulberries, Zelcovas and sweet gums, beeches and Siberian elms still have their leaves. Water striders still hunt in the sloughs. A few daddy longlegs are left in the old wood nettles and touch-me-nots. A few bees and cabbage butterflies still come out, and sometimes moths are drawn to the porch lights at night after the temperatures have rise into the 60s.

Daybook

1982: Fat cabbageworms are eating the garden kale. All the poplar leaves in the yard have fallen except those at the very top; they quiver in the wind.

1983: Cardinal sings at 6:51 a.m. Two buzzards circling along Wilberforce-Clifton Road, the last of the local flock. At South Glen, the weather is windy and misty, high 40s, gray. The canopy is gone except for some oaks, the sycamores, and the Osage orange. Only a few flowers, a late zigzag goldenrod, and a pale purple aster, one autumn violet, then more violets among a patch of henbit. Sweet Cicely, sweet rocket, and garlic mustard foliage growing taller. Goldenrod a burnt brown color. Rose bushes yellowing. Sycamore leaves parachute one by one into the preserve. A parsnip with buds is ready to bloom.

1986: Cardinal sings 6:51 a.m. The ginkgo near Brush Row loses its leaves in a day, a pile of bright gold leaves, thick, leathery soft. Two buzzards seen circling above Grinnell.

1987: All the milkweed in the county seems open. Hedgerow shrubs are gilded in the rain like rows of tall sweet clover or April forsythia in bloom. Apples leaves keep pace with the pussy willow leaves, almost gone. Most Osage foliage is down.

1988: Geese fly over at 8:00 a.m., continue restless through the day. My poplars are blanching but have retained most of their leaves. Half of the winter tomatoes have set fruit, some are now half an inch to an inch in diameter. The first bud appeared on the Christmas cactus yesterday.

1989: Cardinal sings near seven o'clock this morning. Star magnolias: all but a few leaves gone. Sycamores hold along Corry Street. Lil's maple: a third left. Mums hold well to this point in the

year. No killing frost yet. Until a day ago, Madison, Wisconsin had missed the killing frosts, too.

1991: All white mulberry leaves down this morning. First snow flurries, record lows throughout the country.

1992: The garlic that was not dug this summer is starting to grow back in the garden, some spikes an inch or two high. Quince foliage almost all gone. All rose of Sharon down. Oaks go quickly, most of the tree line bare. Uncle Bill says he has six inches of snow on the ground in Gentilly, Minnesota, geese loud there every few minutes, rushing south, he says. Some crickets here in Yellow Springs heard tonight, temperature still in the 60s.

1993: Robins still migrating through South Glen, a small flock seen just past the bridge.

1995: The leaves of the red maple at the park are almost all down, silver maples on Limestone Street are a full palomino gold and beginning to thin.

1999: Yesterday, the ginkgoes were shedding. Today, it's the mulberries, white and red. The back yard fills up with the late-fall leaves, and the barrier between the south garden and the house next door disintegrates. This morning, the first substantial snow of the year, a fourth of an inch on top of yesterday's inch of rain.

2000: Two buzzards seen, maybe the last.

2002: The west red mulberries are gone, as is the box elder beside them. The red quince is pale and thinning. My maple behind the shed is a rich gold and starting to disintegrate, as is the Danielson's maple across the street. The high locusts in back are bare. The ginkgo is down at Xenia Avenue and Herman Street. Susi's Osage fruits are all over the ground; she's no longer there to have Scott roll them down the road.

2003: A cardinal sang at 6:45, a Jenny wren chattering below it in the honeysuckles at the back of the yard. My white mulberry is maybe half yellow now.

2004: The white mulberry, full yellow, started to shed overnight. The red mulberries along the south border are maybe two-thirds down. Robins peeping all around the neighborhood. Starlings clucking nearby. I drove through a huge flock of blackbirds on the way to Cedarville at 10:30 a.m. A doe killed on the highway beyond Jamestown. Green winter wheat noticed for the first time this fall. My ginkgoes at Wilberforce were full gold, half down. Over a dozen buzzards were roosting in a tree above Grinnell Road about 4:15 p.m., five or six others were circling above them as I cam by. At South Glen, winged euonymus was a still a strong rose red through the undergrowth. Nodding smartweed leaves remained pink by the side of the path. One leafcup flower seen.

2005: Screech owl calling at 5:45 this morning. Across the countryside between Yellow Springs and Wilmington, the peak has passed, and silver maples have begun to turn silver and pale palomino gold. In Wilberforce, one ginkgo is down, and the others are shifting to ochre. Along Dayton Street, however, maples are still very bright yellow and orange, Japanese maples deep red. When I was at Greg's house this evening, a small camel cricket appeared by their stairway.

2006: More frost, nights in the 20s, have shriveled most of the hydrangea leaves (except for the oak-leaf hydrangea) and the redbud leaves. Rose of Sharon leaves are almost gone, and honeysuckles are dropping quickly. Rosebuds have finally shriveled. The curly-branched tree in the alley, though, has kept its green leaves – even though they seem brittle. Robins eating berries and starlings singing in the alley at 8:30 a.m.

2007: Light frost continues morning after morning, but the impatiens and the elephant ears have escaped damage so far. In the alley, many orange euonymus berries have emerged overnight. The maple there is almost gone, but a Stafford Street ash is still deep gold. Don's tree held a pair of grackles and a starling. Robins whinnied and moved through the honeysuckles. One junco, the first I've seen, flew over Don's fence as I approached. Now Lil's maple is turning, the Danielsons' is full yellow-orange and shedding, but Mrs. Timberlake's is still green. More leaves coming down throughout town, the peak finally starting to disintegrate.

2009: Crow at 7:01 a.m. Robins peeping in the alley when I walked Bella at about 8:45, one buzzard circling town. Tall coneflowers are finally gone behind the Danielsons'. Some silver maples almost gone. Lil's burning bush has shed all its leaves. Joe Pye tufted. Bridal wreath spirea rusted, thinning.

2010: Robins passing through the neighborhood this morning, Lil's maple losing more leaves, sweet gums holding bright, many ginkgoes shedding, a few completely down, serviceberry trees almost bare, the burning bush throughout the area thinning out, but not gone. In Carl's yard, the bittersweet vine that has climbed maybe twenty feet still has its foliage, keeps gold in the west High Street tree line. Continuing morning frosts have burned back the elephant ears, the Quickweed, the tomatoes, zinnias and most of the impatiens.

2012: Sun, frost, a small flock of starlings whistling and chortling in the High Street trees, robins peeping around me. The beech is in full color, most of the ginkgoes down, mulberries almost gone, squirrels screeching, one squirrel carrying his black walnut across the electrical line over Stafford Street. At Ellis Pond, the sawtooth oak is still green to yellow green. The other oaks are brown but mostly holding their leaves. The hickory trees are bare, and the bald cypress are at least 80 percent gone. All the quince leaves down a few days ago. I tipped them from the net that I had placed over the garden pond. All the burning bush leaves along High Street are down. New England aster leaves staring to yellow.

2013: Crows at 7:05 this morning. Cardinal singing steadily around 9:30. In the alley, the leaves of the bittersweet are a soft gold. Quince leaves hold at half. Burning bush leaves are full red everywhere in town. Now Mrs. Timberlake's maple is about down. Rachel's ginkgo has just started to fade a little. The blueberry bush in the back yard is red and gold. One of Jeanie's yellow tea roses bloomed yesterday; I cut it and brought it in to a vase. And Jeanie's river birch is half soft golden.

2014: Jeanie's river birch in the backyard is turning some, but the leaves did not shrivel or break in the frost. Lil's burning bush is almost bare. All the trees are down on this section of High Street except for Frank's silver maple. Constant robin whinnying all around when I walked Bella near 9:00 a.m., and a small flock of starlings moving through the Stafford Street trees.

2015: Lil's maple shedding now, her burning bush half down (Peggy's still bright). Hackberries and Jeanie's river birch have fallen, and the town ginkgoes have golden skirts at their trunks, but still hold the majority of their leaves. Zelcovas still full, downtown's pear trees are losing only their red eaves, still keep their green and gold. Jeanie's redbud keeps its rich orange-yellow foliage; her blueberry bush still keeps some leaves. The sidewalk redbud is bare, showing off the great spread of bittersweet, berries deep orange. Sycamores along Corry Street are rusty gold considerably thinned.

2017: Inventory after returning from Oregon: Jeanie's river birch is a rich deep gold and retains most of its leaves, dappling the yard; Lil's maple and Mrs. Timberlake's maple are both at full yellow, bookends to the Danielsons' bare maple; Lil's burning bush is deep red; the front sidewalk is slippery from fallen honeysuckle leaves, surprising me with such a sudden collapse of over half its canopy; the star magnolia in front of the "unlucky" house is pale yellow, leaves seeming shrunken but not coming apart; dark clusters of seed pods have replaced the redbuds' ochre leaves with uneven strips of muddy brown; many of the hostas are ceding to age and the chill, turning and bowing; the north viburnum is still deep purple-red and has kept about a third of its leaves; the zinnias stand tight together crisp and withered, their brilliance now a tattered beige; I have cut down most of the castor bean branches that had melted in the frost; the remaining milkweed leaves are mottled olive green and dirty gold, dabs of rust and decay along the edges, still almost soft, their surface feels textured and dusty, perhaps from powdery mildew; the Endless Summer hydrangeas that never bloom are burned and curled at the top; the pokeweed berries continue to dry up, some durable pokeweed leaves still red-orange; always looking to spring, the lungwort and the lamium and the waterleaf grow back strong, rising up fresh out of the decay of the summer plants around them.

2020: Rachel's gingko, which held off turning through October, is suddenly shedding. All the burning bush shrubs of the area are bright but losing leaves.

2021: First killing frost, and the paulownia tree dropped all its leaves at once. The 14-foot castor bean plants have wilted, their gigantic stalks and foliage no defense against the cold. Now maple leaves clatter to the streets and Jeanie's river birch sheds softly into the circle garden. Chris Walker reports turkeys wandering through his property. And Tat sends a photograph of turkeys near the lake in Madison, Wisconsin.

2022: An exceptionally warm start to November, highs in the 60s and 70s so far. One cabbage white emerged over the redbuds as I sat in the yard this afternoon, dove into the zinnias and then headed west across the yard, then disappeared.

The landscape of the Glen brought Herrick to mind, a mix of suggestion, evasion, admission.

Delight In Disorder

A sweet disorder in the dress
Kindles in clothes a wantonness:
A lawn about the shoulders thrown
Into a fine distraction:
An erring lace which here and there
Enthrals the crimson stomacher:
A cuff neglectful, and thereby
Ribbons to flow confusedly:
A winning wave (deserving note)
In the tempestuous petticoat:

A careless shoe-string, in whose tie
I see a wild civility:
Do more bewitch me than when art
Is too precise in every part.

Robert Herrick (1591-1674)

And then another quotation, this from Leon Quel: *Time before the killing frosts and the first inch or two of snow, time before the Osage disappear and all the black walnuts decay and stain the streets and sidewalks, time before the last seeds fall, time before the branches are completely bare on all the trees and shrubs, time before the witch hazels wither....*

And I wrote this week's column for the *News:*

Today at the Covered Bridge, the woods of November in disarray. Between glory and hiddenness, suggestive possibilities.

Most of the branches are bare, but between fullness and emptiness: an attraction of incompletion, allusive remnants of sweet gums and honeysuckles.

Suddenly visible trunks, immodestly revealed, promises budded for the purity of winter's undress. A sweet disorder of fallen leaves, confusing, quivering remainders in the late autumn breeze, warm out of time

The disarray in the sweetness of the vigor of spring and the ripeness of summer and the bold defiance of autumn color.

A reversal of order: leaves out of line, phalanxes of leaves twisted, mismatching, no longer alternate or opposite, no longer clinging or stemmed in rows.

There are empty spaces which memory can't quite reconstruct detritus of things out of sequence, sequences ripped apart sizes altered, no longer clones,

My eye is drawn to the exception, able to single out the exception, the individual, incongruity, harmony in opposites, in loss. But all is also congruent. Now all things are acceptable, and nothing is out of place, everything belongs in detritus, in the great seeding and mulching. There is a simple leveling of magnificence and the commonplace, bright and glowing April green, the fruit of July, October fire: all reshaped.

The sky opens through the canopy, the starkness of the remnants increased by the new angle of the sun, the new access, revealing a great maculation, new dapples and speckles, patches, flecks, spotted, stained.

At the banks of streams and the river, low from the drought of October, the year's cache assembles in islands of leaves, new clusters, new assemblies, new gatherings that create new soft, wet beaches.

2023: Mild bulb planting weather returns after two mornings of hard freeze, Last Monarch butterfly left L:ori' milkwed on October 3. She had nurture eight of them fthrough the summer; they all survived. Many ginkgoes doesn, mamy holding at half. The zelcova by the postoffice remains bright burnt sienna. In the greenhouse, all is settled in. The first Christmas cackus buds are opening, the transplants are settling down, and one canna is blooming, another budded. So the threei or four month greenhouse time is underway, a whole new habitat and season of the year

We'll go nutting once more. We'll pluck the nut of the world and crack it in the winter evenings.... I will take another walk to the Cliff, another row on the river...be out in the first snow, and associate with the winter birds. Here I am at home. In the bare and bleached crust of the earth, I recognize my friend.

Henry David, *Journal*, November 1, 1858

November 4th
The 308th Day of the Year

There is a seasonal exhaustion in the air. The ground is cool and subdued as the hills turn dusky and purple by late afternoon. I pass cleared fields full of stubble, the lank, dark stalks of corn. Milkweeds, where monarchs deposited their eggs, have opened their pods, and the white silk lies over browning grass like wisps of cotton, or is concentrated in spots like the downy feathers of a chicken caught by a fox.

John Hay

Sunrise/set: 7:07/5:30
Day's Length: 10 hours 23 minutes
Average High/Low: 56/37
Average Temperature: 47
Record High: 76 – 2003
Record Low: 17 – 1951

The Daily Weather

Highs reach 70 fifteen percent of the years, are in the 60s another 15 percent, in the 50s twenty-five percent, in the 40s thirty percent, in the 30s ten percent, in the 20s five percent. Light frost comes half of the mornings, hard frost ten percent, rain 40 percent of the days, snow ten percent. After today, thunderstorm activity usually ceases until February, but all-day rains increase.

The Natural Calendar

Throughout the fields and woods, the last autumn violets sometimes still bloom beside a few chicory, Queen Anne's lace, thyme-leafed speedwell, mallow, the final asters. Wild geraniums, thistles, and cinquefoil grow back. Sometimes a parsnip is ready to bloom.

Asparagus fronds and hosta leaves, however, turn yellow in the garden. Along the highways, ironweed and false boneset seeds are soft and pale. Heads of goldenrod and thimbleweed are tufted through the undergrowth, their foliage deep chocolate brown.

The Stars

In the southern sky before midnight, the Pleiades are approaching from the east, Taurus not far behind them. Pisces is due south, Pegasus above it to the west. Fomalhaut, the brightest star of late summer is low on the southwestern horizon. The Big Dipper hugs the northern tree line, the Little Dipper hanging down to the left of Polaris.

Daybook

1983: Ginkgo leaves fall quickly, form a golden mantle under the branches. Rose of Sharon is bare.

1985: One ginkgo by my window is gone, others losing leaves steadily. Lil's maple just starting to turn yellow.

1988: The white mulberry tree in the yard and Lil's maple across the street are now completely bare. Apple, pussy willow and cherry hold at half. The drive to Bowling Green this afternoon was warm and rainy; I traveled through the barometric low that precedes Late Fall. From Yellow Springs north, almost all the trees were down except the green willows, some oaks and stragglers. Most harvest appeared complete.

1989: The major leafdrop is over, and the shock of the change is gone. I am used to the bare branches, and the remaining leaves are no longer fragments of summer but signs of the new season, like blooming trees in April. In the city, gum, willow, and beech are still strong; now the colors shine, gifts of November. The late white mulberry tree in the back yard is suddenly all yellow gold. Most cherry and pussy willows fell in the wind today. A cardinal sang this morning about 7:00, continued off and on until about 8:30.

1990: Tulips planted yesterday in 70-degree temperatures and a soft south wind. Warm again today for digging in the daffodils. It has been the longest autumn. All the late silver maples are palomino gold. The cherry tree is a translucent burnt orange, foliage dropping quickly now. The honeysuckle and quince are dappled. Pear leaves beginning to turn at the edges. Burning bush and barberry still red. The poplar was so bright and gold in the sun yesterday, bending in the wind. Pussy willows: the second set of leaves is green and strong. Robins all around the yard this morning, cardinals, a flicker. Now an aloe has sent up a flower spike in the greenhouse, and five of my indoor tomato plants have filled up the windows in which I placed them. Four other pots are started, sprouts a few inches tall. Late Fall comes with the rain tonight.

1993: In the rain and cold wind, Jeanie's students picked her a big bouquet of dandelions on the way across the golf course this afternoon.

1994: I finally filled the bird feeders two days ago, and the gold finches are here, all brown for winter. The chickadees swoop back and forth to their seeds in the tube feeder, a pair of cardinals feed on the gazebo platform. Out to Dayton this morning: there are plenty of maples still holding, but the tree line is predominantly gray, and there's no doubt that it's Late Fall now (but early Late Fall). At South Glen, the river is clear, slow, and cold, reflecting the gray sky and the black tree trunks, the remnants of golden Osage, red spicebush, yellow-green honeysuckles. It has been a dry fall, and the water is down. The sloping banks are speckled with sycamore and oak leaves. The migrating robins and the turkey vultures have left, and the woods are quiet in the late afternoon. Two mallards, male and female, feed across the river, maybe fifty feet away. They seem indifferent to the danger my dog and I might pose. Are they old or sick? Will they overwinter here like we will? What will the winter bring us?

1995: Uncle Bill called today from northern Minnesota to report the first freeze and the first snowstorm of the year. Gentilly, a thousand miles north west of Yellow Springs, had its first killing frost at the same time as we did here.

1998: The white mulberry in the backyard collapses after a nighttime low in the middle 20s. All day, the yellow-green leaves fall, surrounding the trunk with their soft demise. Across the street, Lil's tree goes quickly, the Danielsons' almost finished. But along

Corry Street, the sycamores hold green and orange, seeming as fresh as they were in October.

1999: One bud still on the water lily in the pond, but only six leaves. The big koi still feed, even though the water temperature is probably in the 40s or low 50s. The woodlots on the way to Dayton were almost bare today, no bright maples or oaks lighting up the horizon. By the roadsides, the honeysuckles and silver olives were yellowing. In town, the beech is becoming red orange.

2001: Some fields plowed for spring between Columbus and Washington Courthouse. Black earth, surrounded by November green, the winter wheat fields glistening in the late afternoon sun.

2002: Robins whinnying in the back yard at sunrise. Dahlias dug this afternoon, old zinnias pulled up. A few spiderworts managed to open today. On the road to Wilmington, the peak has passed, but a certain color density remains. Leaf-fall continues to be intense but has still not pushed the landscape all the way into Late Fall.

2005: One cabbage butterfly seen today. A brown and black woolly bear caterpillar found walking along on the greenhouse floor.

2007: This morning on our walk, Jeanie noticed two of the bittersweet hulls had opened. The bittersweet leaves were a soft, tawny yellow. Long flock of blackbirds or starlings crossed Dayton-Yellow Springs road, flying north as we drove home from shopping.

2008: Sweet gums all red and yellow here in town, full color, along with so many sugar maples and oaks. Judy called to celebrate the election victory last night, mentioned that the annual box elder bug and Asian ladybeetle infestations were at their peak there in Goshen, Indiana. At school today, numerous dandelions were open along the sidewalk.

2009: Thin-leafed coneflowers in full bloom in the alley, and the black-eyed Susans that grow in the yard are also continuing to flower. Some of Don's goldenrod has tufted now, but his latest flowering plants are still rusty. Only two blooms on Peggy's virgin's bower. Among all the trees in the yard, the young South Carolina river birches are holding their color and leaves best of all. Robins whinnying in the yard about 9:00 a.m.

2010: Crows at 7:11 a.m. I found a large camel cricket in the bathtub, the first all year.

2011: Yellow Springs to Gethsemani Abbey, Kentucky: At home, the white mulberry tree is beginning to lose leaves now. Mrs. Timberlake's maple is down, and Lil's and Jimmy's are deep gold and shedding quickly. In the back yard, the river birch is starting to turn all at once. On Dayton Street, the beech is half rusted. By our bedroom window the witch hazel is brown as honey now, and it too is losing leaves. A very different drive from Yellow Springs to Gethsemani, beginning with bright sun and clear skies, ending with gray cumulus and stratus clouds. The roadsides were April green throughout the trip, honeysuckles yellowing, sumac tops red above them. There was no real difference between Ohio and Kentucky in terms of leaf fall: most of the trees were bare, punctuated with russet oaks and glowing maples, red-gold sweet gums and very bright, full ginkgoes, some wood lots still holding, others completely gone. The land continued uniform throughout the trip, Louisville, consequently, not much different from Dayton.

2012: I wake up to leaves from the redbud tree and the white mulberry tree on the lawn where I raked just yesterday. Today, I will just look and listen.

When I am sitting on the porch, I hear two Osage fruits fall into the great open palms of the Lenten roses near the west fence. At the pond, our five koi lie low on the bottom, subdued by the autumn. Pale grape leaves streak the honeysuckle hedge. Even though the hummingbird food slowly disappears, it seems that the bees are the only ones drinking. One white bindweed has blossomed near the trellis, and Ruby's white phlox have a few new flowers. All the finches at the feeders have turned for winter.

Into the woods, the canopy opening in front of me: Zigzag goldenrod and all the asters are half gone; smartweed is blanched by the frost; drifts of snakeroot have gone to seed, brown and gray; deep patches of goldenrod all rusted, flowers and leaves matching now; wood nettle is spotted, drooping; wingstem and ironweed are twisted, sagging, brittle; the pale underside of blackberry leaves turn over in the warm east wind.

This varied, mottled land reflects the motion of the sky, tells the rising of Orion up into the night, this leaf following red Antares, that leaf prophesying Betelgeuse. Open bittersweet along the path uncovers the Milky Way above me. Myopia takes everything in hand. In the glow of ripeness, the stars of November fall around me. Everything is here. All of the facts are in. I need look no further than the undergrowth for Taurus and the Pleiades.

2013: Now the maple on Jerry and Lee's property has finally started to turn. The bur oak at Ellis is pretty much down, and the Zelcovas downtown are rusty brown and shedding. Rob noted that monarch butterflies may be down as much as ninety percent this year.

2014: A call from Bob Barcus this afternoon: He saw a bobcat crossing the bike path today. This is the first time I've received a report about bobcats. Will there be more?

2015: Cypress foliage gone at Ellis.

2016: Cypress foliage half gone at Ellis, most of the sugar maples in the large planting there have shed their leaves. Throughout the countryside, the peak has passed, but many bright sweet gums, maples, Zelcovas and oaks remain, shining in the woodlots and in the suburbs.

2017: Sweet gums near Jill's house: mixed colors red and yellow and orange with green seed pods (a few fallen). In my front hedge, one Japanese knotweed flower protrudes over the sidewalk.

2018: Most of the Champneys' maples, which dominated the street a week ago, are bare. Jill's silver maples are down, but her red maple and sugar maple: full red and gold, Between Frank's house and Mrs. Timberlake's, the star magnolia is deep gold-rust. Lil's burning bush, along with all the others I've seen around the area, is deep scarlet.

The sun was bright all morning, then cirrus filtered the sunlight and cooled the midday. At about one o'clock, I looked into the back yard and saw one male goldfinch, half-gold, sitting alone on the perch of the finch feeder. The usual sparrows and chickadees were nowhere around. The squirrels that almost always haunted the ground in search of bird food were absent.

When I was about to let Monk, the cat, out the back door an hour later, I held back because the finch was still sitting at the feeder, and I was curious about his solitary vigil. Was he sick, ostracized, abandoned, lost? Was he the first or the last of a flock? Was he waiting for another finch? A half hour later, I saw that he had flown to the top of the pole that held the feeder. He was still there after another half an hour, but then he returned to sit at the feeder.

Gradually gray altostratus clouds obscured the Sun, and the breeze picked up. Still the finch waited. Until, when I checked at 3:30, I saw that there were two finches at the feeder. I checked ten minutes later and they both were gone, and I felt a great relief.

I felt relieved, believing that the two might have been looking for each other, or had each been separated from the flock, or that they found each other just at the right time, or that the long wait had ended successfully.

2021: Walk at the Glass farm wetlands, a dozen mallards continuing to hang out on water, and two small, bright yellow sulphur butterflies played around us as we walked about the willows that lined the water. Driving through town, I saw the maples still holding their color, the sweet gums red and purple, the ginkgoes pale yellow green.. Moya's tulip tree is golden brown, Lil's burning bush foliage bright red. The secret maple still glows in the southwestern sunset.

Again the wind
Flakes gold-leaf from the trees
And the painting darkens –
As if a thousand penitents
Kissed an icon
Till it thinned
Back to bare wood
Without diminishment.

Jane Hirshfield, from "The October Palace"

November 5th
The 309th Day of the Year

Whence is it, that the flow'res of the field doth fade,
And lieth buried long in winter's bale?
Yet, soon as spring his mantle hath displayed,
It flow'reth fresh, as it should never fail?

Edmund Spenser

Sunrise/set: 7:08/5:29
Day's Length: 10 hours 21 minutes
Average High/Low: 55/37
Average Temperature: 46
Record High: 77 – 2003, 72 – 2017
Record Low: 12 – 1908

The Daily Weather

This is another pivotal date in the advance of winter: after today, the chances of 70-degree temperatures drop from 15 percent to below five percent. Sixties occur one year in five, 50s one year in two, with 30s and 40s making up the remaining 25 percent. Rain comes 45 percent of the time, snow ten percent. The sun appears just six days in ten.

The Natural Calendar

In warmer years, garlic mustard has grown four or five inches tall, its leaves wide and bright. Chickweed has come back all along the paths, and cress has revived in the pools and streams. Skunk cabbage has pushed up all over the swamp, some plants even opening a little. The low sun sets the new plants glowing like they glow in April. At the river's edge, the water is rippled blue, black, green, and brown, tree branches tangled in reflections.

Warmed by the benign autumn and fed by the great stands of honeysuckle throughout the area, robins linger in town and in the woods. Juncos have arrived, and bluebirds make their last passage south along the Little Miami. Starlings cluck and whistle at sunrise, and cardinals and pileated woodpeckers and bobwhites sing off and on throughout the day. Finches work the sweet gum tree fruits, digging out the seeds from their hollows. Sparrow hawks appear on the fences, watching for mice in the bare fields. Wild turkeys wander through the south end of town.

The last crickets still sing in the warmer evenings, and the last daddy longlegs huddle together in the woodpile. Mosquitoes still wait for prey near backwaters and puddles. Asian lady beetles, more numerous this year than last, look for crevices in which to spend the winter. Late woolly bear caterpillars, most of them dark orange and black, still emerge in the sun. Cabbage butterflies still look for cabbage. Yellow jackets sometimes come out to look for fallen fruit.

Forsythia bushes sometimes bloom a second time when the last bluebirds come through South Glen. Yellow witch hazel graces Dayton Street. Indoors, Christmas cacti are blooming, and the first aloe flower opens in south windows. In a few Yellow Springs gardens, roses, scabiosa, stella d'oro lilies and clematis still blossom.

Hawthorns, crab apples and many honeysuckles are bare, branches marked by red berries left behind, bright against the dull brush. Scarlet rose hips and the buds of pussy willows stand out. Mock orange and forsythia are thinning; their leaf fall measures the progress of the last phase of autumn.

Daybook

1982: My ginkgo leaves fell overnight. First light snow this morning. Red clover seen in bloom along the roadside.

1983: Ginkgo leaves cover the ground, all having dropped overnight, the same night as last year. Osage still yellow green, fruits still thumping to the streets. Some maples still keep their leaves in town; in the country, only the oaks and sycamores stay at all. Violet and white asters still blooming. Cherry trees and pussy willows turning brown. Willows strong and green, poplars also. In Xenia, silver maples almost untouched by the cold.

1985: A pair of buzzards circling alone near South Glen.

1988: At 5:40 p.m., the barometer lies at 29.30, its lowest of the year, the last storm of Middle Fall is moving in for sure. A moth plays in the twilight by the honeysuckle berries in the east garden

1989: Ginkgo leaves cover the ground, fallen overnight, the same as in '82 and '83. Some crickets still sing in the 60-degree evening.

1990: Geese fly over at 5:30 p.m.

1992: First snow at 5:00 a.m. At dawn, the forsythia hedge is bowed and white above, glowing pale green on the lower branches.

1999: Lil's maple almost gone. Ginkgoes and Osage leaves hold at maybe half throughout town. Black pokeberries and red stems stand out against the brown, shriveled leaves below them. Three Shasta daisies are still in bloom, and some small-flowered rudbeckia.

2002: Cardinal at 6:55 a.m. I noticed today that the Korean lilac leaves were completely down. Red burning bush foliage still full. Meal moths, their generation born about October 20th, continue to infest the house.

2003: My ginkgoes in Wilberforce are shedding, but they still have most of their leaves. A little catmint, three yellow roses, some butterfly bush, a few late-seeded purple coneflowers, and five full-blooming scabiosa still flower in the north garden. Two late yellow daylilies in the south garden. Several crows sighted today; I think they're coming back.

2005: The Danielsons' tree is down, and Mrs. Timberlake's is half shed. Lil's maple and Jerry and Lee's hold at the top of their color. The burning bush is shedding by Lil's driveway, and Jerry and Lee's sweet gum is just starting to turn. In the garden, most hostas and astilbe are deep gold and are decaying quickly. The Korean lilac has yellowed and has lost maybe half its leaves. The standard lilacs were hurt by the frost, are half bare. The red mulberry is thinning, and the hackberries have been down for several days. Some stonecrop leaves are yellowing, a rich, full broth color. Along the east fence, two large purple clematis flowers remain open. Jeanie cut a perfect pink rose from along the north wall. In the warm evening, a few tree frogs were whistling. In the southwest, the new moon lay over Dayton with Venus.

2006: Jeanie was shopping near the Dayton Mall, and as she walked across the parking lot, she saw a monarch butterfly flying south.

2007: Soft but blustery morning, purple clouds against Carolina blue sky, against deep orange-golden maples as the barometer falls and a cold wave approaches from Michigan. In Mateo's yard, a few small white asters and chicory flowers still bloom. Lil's maple is half turned now, and silver maples are shades of palomino tan all along the highway. My ginkgoes at school are all turning pale ochre. Korean lilac leaves are a weak yellow green, maybe thinned out by half. A few snow flurries in the afternoon. Several Christmas cacti blossoms open in the greenhouse.

2008: Yet another sunny, warm day in the low 70s. Lil's tree is half down, Danielsons' almost all down, Mrs. Timberlake's was half down this morning, mostly all down by the end of the day, the maple in Jerry and Lee's yard full color and starting to shed. Along Xenia Avenue, a few pear trees are red. The beech on Dayton Street has started to rust. The chinquapin oak across from Don's house is all golden. Mateo's elm is yellow gold, and the Zelkova near the post office. The alley's panicled dogwood is breaking down into rust and yellow and mauve. As I walked Bella through the alley, a squirrel dropped an apple near us from the apple tree; I had thought the apples were all down, but the squirrel had either found one hanging from the branches or had brought one up from the ground and was taking it home. At Earth Rose, Ed Oxley mentioned seeing a large flock of crows along East Enon road yesterday. Ruby came by in the afternoon, talked about her grandson counting 52 buzzards last week, described a golden maple in front of a red oak in the neighbor's yard, gold framed in scarlet.

2009: A mild and quiet morning, robins absent, waning moon in the haze. In the alley, the bridal wreath spirea has lost many of its leaves, rust and gold.

2010: Mornings are frosty now, the days dry and sunny. Throughout the countryside, silver maples have turned palomino gold and dominate the city landscape; the burning bush has lost most of its leaves; staghorn sumac is also bare, but its horns keep red in the thickets; honeysuckles, yellow-green, still give life to the undergrowth; redbuds are almost bare; pussy willows have no leaves, but so many catkins are showing; the pink quince leaves (pale yellow) have filled the pond. Across the street, Lil's maple is deep ochre, about two-thirds shed, her burning bush almost gone. In the greenhouse, mother-in-law's-tongue has a two-foot flower stalk with white buds, and Christmas cacti have long orange buds.

2011: Gethsemani Abbey: Sun, not a cloud overhead, crisp, cool. The ginkgo tree in the monastery courtyard was full gold when I arrived yesterday. Today it is almost all down, its foliage ceding to the cold front that arrived behind the low clouds. Most sweet gum trees on the church grounds have lost about three-fourths of their leaves. I saw a mocking bird on the wall by the monks' graves, hunting for insects or seeds. Only crows in the distance and a long cardinal call, but none of the music I heard this September from the mocking bird.

2012: All the rest of the white mulberry leaves collapsed in the frost last night, but the Osage still holds pretty well. Silver maples and sweet gums are shedding in town, silver maple leaves curling up in the cold.

2013: Distant crows at 6:50 this morning. Lee and Jerry's maple and Jeanie's river birch now almost full color. The white mulberry tree is still green, but the honeysuckle bushes in front of the house are three-fourths down.

2014: Another soft morning, clouds, 40s. Distant crows, robins still passing through the neighborhood in the bare hackberries and maples, chirping of starlings, the cluck of a grackle. There seems to be a pause now, the leaves down, the deeper cold still to come, the robins either continuing to migrate or continuing to scout this area for overwintering like the small flocks of starlings that are common through the coldest months.

2015: Today was a rare day in the 70s throughout the eastern half of the nation, a light breeze from the south, clouds and sun. At the edge of the grocery store parking lot, Kathy pointed out the fallen persimmons, picked some up and ate them on the spot. Above us, the high tree, leaves gone, was full of the small, red fruits.

2016: Very light frost this morning with fog; the zinnias, elephant ears and castor beans remained unhurt. Throughout the countryside, flocks of crows and starlings in the cutover soybean fields. Mrs. Timberlake's maple is about three-fourths bare, and Jill's maple came down several days ago. Frank's maple has thinned out, and about all the hackberry leaves have shriveled or fallen. Along the main street in town, ginkgoes are full gold, starting to shed.

2017: Mild and humid middle 60s this morning. Storm on the way. A cardinal, crows and robins heard after sunrise. A medium-size flock of crows few west over the house at midmorning. Lil's and Mrs. Timberlake's and Jerry and Lee's maples are thinning, but still dominant gold along the street. Frank's silver maple: gray-palomino. Rachel's ginkgo a powdery, guacamole green. Lil's burning bush violent red! Jeanie's river birch and the pond quince are dusky yellow and more fragile now. More honeysuckle leaves, pale dun and soft, cover the front sidewalk, more hostas melting, ochre with age. Day lily foliage has deteriorated at about the same rate as the hostas, not ready to cut off yet. Daisy plants are strong and green. Purple-red pokeweed against the rich mustard of the ancient peach tree. In the garden, celandine flowering, chickweed budded. At the Glass Farm wetland, long drifts of water willows all deep golden in the half-sunlight, a few dandelions and queen Anne's lace and small white asters, two sulphur butterflies and two common buckeyes. At the Catholic graveyard, white oaks deep magenta.

The wind was warm throughout the afternoon, bringing the temperature to 72. Tonight, the longest thunderstorm I can remember, over an hour long, three and a quarter inches of rain – a whole month's precipitation. Full moon at perigee from the 4th through today brought significant weather to complement the second cold front of the month.

2018: Mild and mostly sunny: I noticed all the locust leaves have come down, and the north yard is filling with hackberry leaves.

2020: Crows at 7:05 this morning, sky streaked with bright pink. Moya's tulip tree is finally thinning, as is Lil's maple. And half of the Dayton Street beech is rusty orange. Mild, sunny weather continues, high in the upper 60s, and is expected to last until the 11th. Hurricane Eta ravages Nicaragua and heads toward Cuba and southern Florida.

2021: John Blakelock reports surprise at two of his Jack-in-the-pulpits emerging after the warm October..

2022: Warm, cloudy, gusty winds, gibbous moon waxing almost full, late leaves blown down, the Dayton Street beech half down, Peggy's pear tree thinned to half. And Maddie and Amy reported the arrival of over two dozen juncos. When they looked out their window, they thought the land looked like it was jumping up and down, but it was the flock feeding and shifting. Jill talked about murmurations of leaves walking down the street in a flash dance, choreographed by the wind.

2023: Mild, sun. All the downtown zelcovas are still rich burnt-sienna, many ginkgoes, beeches, late sugar maples and sugar gums still holding on, but my tulip tree at Moya's house is almost gone. In the greenhouse: a wonderful early November stability: one new canna blossom, one canna budding, one red Christmas cactus opening, a few geraniums and vincas flowering. And the foliage is still October fresh. Even the broad-leafed tropical trees from Jill are keeping their foliage.

Changed is the season, and the time is hard:
And already Arcturus dives into the midst of the waves;
And the sun, who hides from us, has quenched his rays;
And the winds go muttering through the air;
Nor do I yet know how or when will summer return.

Jacopo Sannazaro

November 6th
The 310th Day of the Year

Time may be too short for our Designs...
The World itself seems in the wane.

Sir Thomas Browne

Sunrise/set 7:09/5:28
Day's Length: 10 hours 19 minutes
Average High/Low: 55/37
Average Temperature: 46
Record High: 78 - 1975
Record Low: 19 – 1908

The Daily Weather

November 6th brings a five percent chance of 70s, a 10 percent chance of a high in the 60s and a 40 percent chance of 50s; chillier 40s, however, occur 35 percent of the days, and highs just in the 30s come 10 percent of the time. Odds are better for clouds than sun: on this date the skies are clear to partly cloudy only 40 percent of the years. There is frost this morning 45 percent of the years in my record. Rain occurs 30 percent of the days, snow on 15 percent.

The Natural Calendar

Most of the milkweed pods have opened. A few blackberry bushes are bare; others are still red and purple. Mums are past their best, but the witch hazels are usually still flowering.

Daybook

1982: All the white mulberry leaves are gone, down in a single day. Comfrey is still green and strong. New burdock, two feet tall, is bright emerald green. Most grape leaves have fallen. Raspberry leaves are dark gray and withered.

1986: Cardinal heard at 9:02 a.m.

1987: The woods were so quiet today, Late Fall must have come last night. Mock orange thinning. Pecan gone. No fish biting at

Sycamore Hole.

1988: First snow, one inch, as Late Fall pushes through with a sudden plunge in barometric pressure.

1990: Yesterday, a huge low-pressure system cut away the last ridge of Middle Fall. All my magnolias at school fell together, lay in a pile by the west door. The ginkgoes outside my window turned between the 2nd and the 5th, and then they all came down today in 40 mph gusts. Late leaf-drop is finally taking place almost everywhere. Even Lil's stubborn maple shed all its leaves today. Only the white mulberry is holding. Geese flew over 5:20 p.m.

1992: Late Fall came today, an inch of snow, wet, heavy flakes, highs only in the 30s.

1993: Skirts of gold all around the ginkgoes at Wilberforce today.

1995: Ginkgo leaves fell all at once last night. At home, the red mulberries and the rose of Sharon leaves along the south edge of the property have come down within the past two or three days, all the summer's privacy now gone.

2000: Red oak down at school, English oak almost half shed, ginkgo three fourths. At 4:45 p.m. as I leave, hundreds of crows fly over, probably heading home for the night. In the yard, red mulberry, rose of Sharon, quince half to three-fourths fallen.

2002: Cardinals singing back and forth at 6:55 a.m., the sky clear, 32 degrees. South to Wilmington: still very strong color. We are maybe at October as far as "average" foliage conditions are concerned.

2003: Throughout the countryside, most of the leaves are down except for bright yellow Osage, a few yellow maples, a few brown oaks.

2004: Robins were migrating through the yard this morning. Starlings filled the back trees at noon.

2005: One of the large jade trees in the greenhouse started to bloom this morning.

2006: In the middle of all the fallen leaves near the shed, one violet cyclamen continues to bloom. Jerry and Lee's sweet gum tree has all its color and is starting to shed a little; the soft maples in the alley are half down; the Dayton Street beech tree is just about full gold. No buds on the jade trees this year. A cardinal sang this morning at 7:00. Robins still heard peeping in the back woods. Moya said she saw a pheasant between our yards one afternoon last week. Could it have been a turkey?

2007: Black walnuts are falling quickly from the Limestone tree, and two of Mateo's last four came down yesterday. Temperatures finally have fallen below normal, and frost comes almost every morning. Lil's tree is in full color now, and the Danielsons' is full and almost half down; Mrs. Timberlake's is almost full. Sparrows are ravenous at the feeders. Starlings sit in Don's tree most every morning, starling chatter throughout the alley. Two yellow tea roses cut from the garden last week continue bright, wide open.

2008: Paying attention to where and when the sunlight comes through my window helps me to feel cared for. Strangely, it makes me feel chosen.

When I watch it, I feel like I am not only following time made visible and measurable right on my wall, but I am also finding a place for myself in the Sun.

My relationship with the Sun is different when I am outside. Out in the yard or the woods or on the road, the Sun has no limits. It shines everywhere, belongs to everything and to every creature.

But when I am inside watching in my room, the Sun is more intimate. It is not so vast and almighty. Instead, it seems a bright blessing for me. I am the only one who sees it here. It is a light for solitude and courage and an ally against the winter ahead.

2009: Mrs. Timberlake's giant silver maple is the only tree on the block holding so steadily, a palomino golden green. Crows at 7:30, robins peeping this morning around 8:30. No starlings heard or seen until the middle of the day when a whole flock swooped down onto our honeysuckle bushes and gobbled berries.

2010: Crows at 7:09 a.m., robins peeping after sunrise. Roses at the Korean restaurant in Fairborn in full bloom. Sweet gums and ginkgoes continuing to shed, but many of them have most of their leaves. Matt called from down the street about 9:30 this morning, said he and Jennifer had heard some kind of geese or cranes calling when they went outside. Matt didn't think they were Canadian geese, and it is too early (I believe) for sandhill cranes. And when I played a recording of the sandhills for him, he didn't think that was the right sound. Turkeys, perhaps.

2011: To Yellow Springs from Gethsemani in Kentucky, sun and 60 degrees all the way: The landscape mostly bare throughout the trip, more leaves actually appearing the further north (and the further into suburban plantings) I drive. Oaks are the most prominent holdouts along the way. In Kentucky, one monarch killed as I was slowing down for construction. Another monarch butterfly seen crossing (higher) the highway near Dayton. Buzzards sighted off and on throughout the trip, six deer road kills by the side of the freeway. At home, the quince leaves have filled the garden pond; about half of them remain .

2012: The silver maple at Ellis Pond has shed its leaves, clusters of ruddy buds prominent now. All of the bald cypress trees have dropped their foliage, and only the sawtooth oak and the willow by the edge of the water have kept green leaves. Throughout town, all of the ginkgoes have fallen, and even the Dayton Street beech tree is losing leaves. No more mice coming to the traps in the greenhouse: three voles and three field mice were the total.

2013: Lil's burning bush started to shed dramatically overnight. Intense leaf fall throughout the village, ginkgoes poised to come down, full gold. Over half the quince foliage fell to the pond in the afternoon wind and rain.

2014: Robins still whinnying in the morning throughout the neighborhood.

2015: Another day in the low 70s, robins whinnying, quince foliage down but lilacs and elm holding out so I can't really take the netting from the pond. Lil's burning bush bare, her maple just keeping a few shriveled leaves. My Osage is gold and shedding early. The white mulberry trickles down. One hundred snow glories planted, 80 windflowers today, and 120 tulips yesterday, 75 daffodils last week. Chickadees and titmice constantly feeding. Numerous buzzards circling Xenia Avenue in the afternoon. Ed Oxley reported seeing a giant flock of blackbirds north of town – the first report I've had of the great gatherings this fall.

2016: Sun and mild, light breeze: In the zinnias, honeybees, a large bumblebee, a painted lady and a pearl crescent. No quince leaves down yet, Lil's burning bush holding all its leaves, her maple still full gold. Intense feeding at the bird feeders, chickadees, the red-bellied woodpecker, a blue jay, cardinals, titmice, sparrows. At the grocery store parking lot, all the persimmon leaves are down, but the branches are still full of dusky-rose fruit.,

2017: Late Fall arrives on schedule, cold after last night's rain.

2018: The sun was bright all morning, and then wispy "mare's tails" cirrus clouds filtered the sunlight and cooled the midday. Late Fall was due, with wind and rain. At about one o'clock, I looked into the back yard and saw one male goldfinch, half-gold, sitting alone on the perch of the finch feeder. The usual sparrows and chickadees were nowhere around. The squirrels that almost always haunted the ground in search of bird food were absent.

When I was about to go out the back door an hour later, I held back because the finch was still sitting at the feeder, and I became curious about his solitary vigil. Was he sick, ostracized, abandoned, lost? Was he the first or the last of a flock? Was he waiting for another finch? What was he feeling? A half hour later, I saw that he had flown to the top of the pole that held the feeder. He was still there after another half an hour, but then he returned to sit at the feeder fifteen minutes later.

Gray altostratus clouds slowly obscured the sun. The storm was moving closer. Still, the finch waited. Until, when I checked at 3:45, I saw that there were two half-turned, male goldfinches at the feeder. I looked out at 4:00, and they both were gone.

Later that afternoon, the storm that would take down all ginkgo leaves brought the dark in early. And I felt relieved for the first finch. Maybe he had been overcome by a crisis of solitude or by fear of being alone just as cruel weather threatened. Maybe the second finch had come just in time.

I realize now that my interest had less to do with the solitary goldfinch than with my own emotions. In my ignorance of what may be common finch behavior, I projected my own anxieties upon the visitor. I made up an existential story to fit my nervousness at the approach of Late Fall. Embarrassed about that, I composed an odd koan to chide my feelings: "What is the meaning of one goldfinch waiting?"

2020: Another day of sun and warmth in the 60s, robins peeping all around the yard, Carolina wren song at dawn. Sulphur butterflies and grasshoppers in the path beyond the pond.

2021: The High Street ginkgoes have collapsed from the frosts, but the white mulberry tree still holds green. Honeysuckle leaves clutter the sidewalk in front of the house. I planted the last of the 175 tulips in the north and east yard. New moon and perigee have kept the barometer high and the nights cold.

2022: Blustery and mild, and a late cabbage white butterfly came by from High Street, over the redbud and the bittersweet.to explore what might be left. Leah saw a painted lady on her butterfly bush.

2023: Robins still peeping in the bushes. Buzzards still circling south of town. Leaves have piled up: time to bring them to the garden.

There are no fixed limits,
Time does not stand still.
Nothing endures,
Nothing is final.
The game is never over,
Summer and winter,
Birth and deathmAre even

Chuang Tzu (from Thomas Merton

It is rarely that an artist succeeds in painting unmistakably the difference between sunrise and sunset; and it is equally a trial of his skill to put upon canvas the difference between early spring and Late Fall.

John Burroughs

Sunrise/set: 7:11/5:27
Day's Length: 10 hours 16 minutes
Average High/Low: 54/36
Average Temperature: 45
Record High: 76 – 1938, 73 – 2020
Record Low: 20 – 1903

The Daily Weather

Highs in the 70s occur five percent of the time on this date. Ten percent of the afternoons reach into the 60s; forty percent make the 50s; thirty-five percent make the 40s; ten percent rise only into the 30s. Skies are overcast 45 percent of the time, and freezing temperatures strike four days out of ten. Rain falls only 25 percent of the days; snow comes about one day in ten.

The Natural Calendar

The middle of second spring marks this time of year. When the temperature reaches 60, and cardinals sing, and the starlings cluck in the high trees, November seems like April. Waterleaf is strong on the slopes. Celandine often blooms in the garden, along with a few dandelions, some roses, some chickweed, some violets, deadnettle and wild strawberries. Seeds sprout in rotting logs.

Daybook

1982: Periwinkle emerges from the brown leaves in the wind. Dandelions, wild mallow still in bloom, Osage leaves thinning, golden. Honeysuckle leaves offer the only green in the woods. Japanese honeysuckle in the front yard appears to be unaffected by the cold.

1983: Ginkgoes hang on outside my office window. Lil's tree still has half its leaves.

1984: Lil's tree is yellow green, still has almost all its leaves.

1985: Late ginkgoes almost solid yellow, and strong. Many late maples also full yellow.

1986: Cardinal sings at 8:10 a.m. Peach leaves all gone. Cherry tree gold and green, half shed, Osage dropping leaves quickly, Lil's maple has collapsed. Chubs steal bait at Sycamore Hole. The high canopy is down except for the Osage. Fields are gray with goldenrod seeds. Huge flock of geese flies over the Glen at 5:21 p.m. A few crickets are singing.

1988: Now the pussy willow is half thinned, cherry is down and the apple. Sudden leaf-fall on my honeysuckles: branches of orange berries against the last yellow maple.

1990: The last honeysuckle, dogwood, spicebush, boxwood, elms, sugar maples, garlic mustard, sweet Cicely, yarrow, and aster leaves glow with an April light. Altogether, they produce in me a feeling of renewal without the trauma of winter, a sudden reprieve. I look down into the valleys toward Yellow Springs Creek, and I feel the hope of spring, with none of its demands.

1993: Last night, after more cold and more snow, the white mulberry leaves came down, punctuating the punctual arrival of Late Fall. I collected most of the last mums from the south garden this morning, and Jeanie made bouquets for the whole house. The final roses were cut along the north garden wall, a red, a pink, and a yellow.

2001: The quince is yellow green and more than half down. The lilac has been hurt by the frost, its leaves shriveled and dark. The Korean lilac's foliage is completely gone, after shedding through the end of October. The beeches on High and Dayton streets have their full, rich rusty color now, but the tree line in the countryside is leaner, more maples and ginkgoes down. The roadside grass seems paler too.

2003: Cardinal song at 6:45 this morning. The wren chattered at the same time. Then, as usual, silence. I haven't heard blackbirds or starlings the past couple of mornings. In the past few days the pink quince and the west red mulberry have come completely undone. Lil's maple only keeps its withered brown leaves. Tonight, a medium-sized green cricket-like creature with wings, something like a cross between a cricket and a katydid, flew and sat beside me as I worked at the greenhouse table. She had escaped the deadly cold forecast for tonight. I talked to her about the flowers and the plants around us, the benefits of this paradise.

2004: A soft day, high near 60, sky perfectly blue. I was cutting the last zinnias and Mexican sunflowers when a monarch butterfly came south over Mrs. Lawson's fence. (Note: Reviewing my monarch sightings between 1982 and 2014, this November 7th monarch is the last of the monarchs observed.)

2006: The spirea leaves are turning now, some red, some gold. Hosta leaves melting quickly into the ground. Some pear trees starting in Wilmington as beeches deepen. Robins still peeping throughout the day. I found a small camel cricket in the bathtub last night before I went to bed; it was gone in the morning.

2007: A flock of dark-eyed juncos were in the alley this morning as I walked through with Bella.

2008: Robins in the morning for the past few days. Now a rapid descent into Late Fall, Lil's maple and burning bush coming down rapidly. All the other sugar maples except Lee and Jerry's are bare. The pears downtown are turning gold and red, the beech is gathering color. Honeysuckles have turned solid bright yellow and are now losing leaves, the shrub line thinning all around the yard. At school yesterday, my gingkoes were all golden and half shed.

2009: Driving home from Leesburg, sun setting, then red sky all the way to Yellow Springs: The leaves are gone throughout the countryside, some cornfields and soy fields stand, but most of the land is bare.

2010: A heavier frost this morning, and the white mulberry foliage has been clattering down all day. The last foliage of Lil's maple has withered more, is poised to fall. Starlings throughout the east trees along Stafford Street when I walked Bella at about 11:00. No crickets heard this evening.

2011: Most of the ginkgoes in town are holding full gold. Lil's maple and Jimmy's more about two-thirds down. Zelcovas in town are shedding quickly, down to about half their leaves. Mild weather brought out one cabbage white, many bees. The pond is filling with quince leaves. A few soft, lisping cricket songs (field crickets) tonight, intermittent, weak.

2012: A flock of crows seen today in the soybean field on the west edge of town. Only leafcup, a few columbine and hepatica leaves, sweet rocket and garlic mustard basil clusters, and the first skunk cabbage spears of 2013 showing at the base of the north Glen stairway.

2013: In the last two days, all the bittersweet hulls have opened, revealing the fruit deep orange. Now Lil's maple is three-fourths down – catching up with the quince. Frank's silver maple coming along quickly, the Dayton Street beech full turned, more pears burnished. All of Carl's maples are gone. Jerry and Lee's maple suddenly coming apart. No robins or starlings heard on my walk this morning.

2014: The Dayton Street beech full gold, russet, yellow, thinning some. Peggy's limelight hydrangea a rusted brown, all its flowers holding. Her burning bush, and the barberries over at Al's are half gone. The foliage of the Japanese knotweed remain attached to their stalks, brittle, almost translucent. The fallen leaves of a ginkgo across the street are dulling pale now, their brilliant skirt around the tree trunk starting to blend with the ground. By the old train station, the columnar English oak is still green, only a little weathering.

2016: I rest in a blue lawn chair in the afternoon sun looking at the zinnias that have survived to this point in the autumn. One buzzard is sailing above me in the clear sky. Around the zinnias, flowers of the New England asters are gray, round tufts of seeds. Only a few light frosts have occurred so far this month, and the elephant ears and castor bean plants remain vigorous. I am watching for butterflies and bees, nursing a small water glass of white wine.

First comes the silver-spotted skipper, inconspicuous brown, fitting easily with the browning leaves and stems of the zinnias. A few bumblebees travel from flower to flower, lighting for only a moment before moving on. Then a bright yellow sulphur rises out of the bushes and flies to the top of the wisteria that has grown across the garden trellis, remaining there to bask in the sun.

Then comes a cabbage white zigzagging across the tops of the flowers, uninterested, it seems, to land and check for flowers. Behind me on the bird feeders, the sparrows cluster, then burst up at the smallest sound, then fly back to eat, then explode again, then fly back again. As I am about to leave, a female deer moves quietly through the wooded border between my yard and Moya's just a few yards from me. Along Xenia Avenue, the ginkgoes are still bright gold, only shedding a little. The sweet gums have become tattered, but are still red and yellow.

2017: Jon Whitmore called at 9:20 this evening to say he had heard what were probably sandhill cranes: "We think we just heard a good omen, there were creatures flying through the night sky, jabbering along, and it was some kind of crane, didn't remind me that much of the sandhill cranes, but certainly sounded like cranes."

2018: A robin peeping when I cam outside at about 8:30. Lil's tree is about bare except for a few leaves withered by the frost, but her burning bush and many red maples and Japanese maples are still bright and intact. The remaining High Street maples are pretty well gone. The Dayton Street beech, the red oaks and the pear trees in town are a full burnished golden, burnt-sienna. Many sycamores have thinned but keep their rusty gold. The frost of the next two days should bring down the ginkgoes. Two small daffodil beds planted near the north trellis.

2019: Back from two weeks in Europe (in which both Amsterdam and Paris were in deep early autumn color.) Here, the secret maple, the Danielsons' maple, Moya's maple, many of the sugar maples, and about all the ashes at Ellis are down, with many silver maples leaves fallen around the pond. Cypress trees are browning at the water's edge. No geese seen in the afternoon, the day blustery and cold. Lil's maple is full gold, her burning bush scarlet all the way. In the north garden, the viburnum is almost completely fallen. The Virginia creeper that had invaded the greenhouse has turned like the vines outside. Jill reports several murmurations of starlings in the fields between the village and Fairborn. When we walked to the graveyard at 5:30, two sizeable and vociferous flocks of geese flew over out from the gold-gray horizon. In the greenhouse, the first white Christmas cactus had put out small buds.

2020: Sunny and 73 degrees: Jogging toward the old tree beyond Ellis Pond, I watched cabbage whites and sulphurs and grasshoppers in the lush green path beside the uncut cornfield. Geese were feeding on the other side of the road, tucked into to long grass. Few starlings in town this fall, a few murmurations in the fields, but I wonder if there has been a decline overall in their numbers.

I cannot think of any individual as existing except as part of a pattern - and the pattern's most visible and tangible areas are of course the individual's immediate environment: the soil and culture-stream from which he springs, and the milieu of ideas, impressions, traditions, landscapes, and architecture, through which he must necessarily peer in order to reach the "outside."

H. P. Lovecraft

Absence and presence are complementary, are two aspects of the same reality. Death or ending is the mirror of life or beginning. Absences fill the deceptive pods of presence, create wholeness from the parts that seem so transitory or so broken but are only incomplete.

bf

Sunrise/set: 7:12/5:26
Day's Length: 10 hours 14 minutes
Average High/Low: 54/36
Average Temperature: 45
Record High: 73 – 1975, 80 – 2020
Record Low: 17 – 1971

The Daily Weather

The weather today is generally warmer than it was yesterday: chances of highs in the 60s increase to 30 percent (70s coming infrequently at 4 percent, 80s only once in a century), often because of the approach of a low-pressure trough preceding the month's third cold front. Thirty percent of the highs are in the 50s, twenty-five percent are in the 40s, ten percent in the 30s. Sixty-five percent of the time, mornings stay above freezing. Clouds cover the sky three days in ten; the chances of rain are 30 percent, of snow ten percent.

The Weather in the Week Ahead

Late Fall almost always arrives by this second week of November. It is a transition season during which the last leaves fall, skies darken, wind speed increases, hard frosts put and end to the year's flower and vegetable cycles, and farmers complete harvest.

High-pressure systems, accompanied preceded by clouds and rain or snow, typically cross the Mississippi River around the 9th and the 1p. The 9th is historically the wettest day of November's second week. The 11th and 12th are the sunniest, and the 13th is the driest. One partly cloudy afternoon in the 60s or 70s comes six years out of ten during this time of the year, but cold and precipitation are the norm.

The Natural Calendar

Many of the Osage orange, silver maples, oaks, beeches, pears, and sweet gums continue to hold their leaves. Most ginkgoes have collapsed, however, and the last white mulberry foliage comes down if the frost is heavy. On this date in 1984, Evelyn Hatton, correspondent for the *Switzerland Democrat* in Vevay, Indiana (in southern Indiana along the Ohio River), wrote: "It's pawpaw, persimmon and sweet potato time. You might include squirrel hunting plus walnut and hickory nut gathering."

By the end of the week, Procyon of Canis Major is just over the horizon at 11:00 p.m. The Great Square has moved into the western half of the sky, Cygnus leading the way. Winter's Pleiades are well up in the east, followed by Aldebaran and the constellation Taurus. Cassiopeia is now due south of Polaris.

Daybook

1982: A few nights ago the temperature in my yard dropped into the middle 20s. At 7:30 in the morning, I looked out the back door as the Sun was coming up over the houses on High Street: I saw the leaves of my white mulberry tree starting to fall.

I was excited because I had never witnessed the total collapse of the mulberry. I had kept sporadic track of that particular tree's history, and I knew it always lost its foliage in early November. But I had never actually seen the leaves come down all at once.

So now I watched while the branches hemorrhaged, leaves clattering down in sheets, in gusts, for almost an hour. At 8:30 the tree was empty, and the ground was covered.

Trying to understand what I'd witnessed, I went out and counted the number of leaves in a square foot beneath the tree: 65 leaves large and small filled the space. I measured the area that held most of the newly fallen leaves: 55 by 40 square feet. I multiplied, came up with 2,200 square feet, multiplied that times 65 leaves per square foot. I had seen around 143,000 leaves come down. Give or take maybe 50,000. Divided by 50 minutes: about 3,000 leaves a minute.

The next morning, I found that the ginkgo near my window had shed all its leaves overnight. I went outside and counted again. There were about 100 ginkgo leaves in a square foot, all lying in an area about 35 feet by 35 feet: my math produced a little more than 122,000 leaves.

Why did I do that? I suppose the numbers are one way of trying to face the enormity of the end of summer. Counting is an attempt to touch and to hold elusive frames of time, to notice them instead of to ignore them, to literally bring down to earth and to sum up the effect of the changing tilt of the planet, to set a mirror to presence as well as to absence, to face autumn and the meaning of autumn and to see that they are material and finite, countable.

1983: All flowers gone in the North Glen. High oaks keep their chocolate-brown leaves. Maples and ginkgoes hang on at about half in the village. Thin-leafed waterleaf has grown back strong, ready for spring.

1984: The late ginkgoes on Brush Row and on Dayton Street are gold and holding. Celandine, chicory and cheeses still bloom in the yard, and hemlock by the west border. Forsythia has been blooming in the east row for a week or so. Osage leaves are yellowing, as are the white mulberry. Kale and chard are still thriving in the changeable weather: one day frost, then rain, a day in the 70s, then one in the 30s. The grass is still growing.

1985: Robin seen near Wilberforce. Starlings chirp most of the days. Late ginkgoes lose more leaves, and all but a few magnolia leaves are gone. Our cherry is turning brown at the edges.

1986: Ginkgo near full yellow. Autumn violets still bloom. Silver maples about half gone. The rest of the tree line is bare except for the Osage (a third to half gone) and a few late sugar maples, some of which are still full color.

1987: Branches essentially bare throughout the area. Only willows and a few Osage hold. Crickets still sing late in the evening after eight of the warmest November days in the last decade.

1988: Zigzag goldenrod leaves are purple brown, the flowers gone to seed.

1990: Cold and clear. Starlings flocking along Wilberforce-Clifton, woolly bear caterpillars crossing the black road, which has warmed in the morning sun. Most all the white mulberry leaves fell last night after a hard freeze of 24 degrees.

1992: Blue jays heard in the back woods. One impatiens is still blooming next the house. Blue flag foliage yellows now, rapid honeysuckle leaf fall.

1993: A cardinal sang at 6:55 this morning.

1997: This morning, a cardinal sang when I walked outside a little after 7:00 a.m. One cricket chirped for a few seconds, then there was just the sound of the wind and the cars on the freeway six miles west. The maples have held on all week - even the weak front yard maple is only half fallen. A bouquet of pink and violet achillea picked this morning, and a purple four-petal mystery plant (maybe money plant) that has survived the frosts to bloom in November. Some Siberian iris transplanted this afternoon, and the north hedge cut back to allow more room for flowers. This afternoon in the wind, I sat and watched gusts of leaves flying over the roof into the pond.

2000: Chicory and celandine, white and red clover, dandelion, early witch hazel all in bloom. One cricket was chanting in the rain at 11:00 p.m.

2001: One field cricket singing in the cold at 6:15 p.m.

2002: My shed-window sugar maple still holds. Lil's maple holds. Red mulberry blackened by the frost, rose of Sharon shriveling. Butterfly bush still green, but honeysuckles are losing ground, and the bamboo is becoming lightly mottled.

2003: This morning after a freeze of 25 degrees, the yellow upper leaves of the white mulberry began to clatter to the ground as soon as the sun warmed their stems. A rush of leaves, sudden autumn, no equivocation.

2004: All the ginkgoes are down at Wilberforce except for the one by my office window – it is holding at about a third.

2005: Honeysuckle yellowing, redbuds all down, my ginkgo at school full yellow, many sweet gums along the way to Wilmington are red and strong, poplars gold and three-fourths gone.

2006: In the front garden, snow-on-the-mountain is coming back, starting to replace the yellowing, wilting leaves of the sedum. The honeysuckle at the front arbor is almost bare, but the honeysuckle hedge along the north property line still keeps out Dayton Street. Lil's maple holds just a handful of leaves. In the greenhouse, I have three tomatoes, each about an inch across, and the Christmas cacti are all in totally full bloom.

2007: A cardinal sang in the twilight of 6:55 this morning. The trees along the road to Wilmington had passed peak color over the past weekend, but many still hold their leaves.

2008: One cardinal song when I walked Bella in the alley about 8:30 this morning. One Christmas cactus plant is in full bloom, but the other plants are in decline, one not even budded. Snow yesterday across the Dakotas. Windy here today, 40s and cloudy, but I planted crocus along the front walk. Shedding leaves continue to open the way to Late Fall. The yellow foliage of the small, new river birches came down overnight. In the Caribbean, Hurricane Paloma – a Category 4 – threatens Cuba.

2009: The sunset as I came back from Leesburg tonight was not the deep red of last night but rather red-peach blending to pale blue gray. And a few clouds lay across the west, not like last night's pure clarity.

2010: Lil's tree hangs on at about a tenth or so. Jerry and Lee's maple is still full, as is Burl's young maple. Downtown, near the post office and along Dayton Street, the Zelcovas keep their most of their red-orange leaves, only the tops of the trees shedding. The river birch in the backyard is yellowing but still keeps most of its leaves. Half of the white mulberry leaves came down yesterday. The other half – which belong to its sister tree – remain. Along the road south, the tree line is bare except for occasional oaks. The silver maples hold in town, but are rare in the countryside. Along Xenia Avenue, all but one of the ginkgoes are down, as is Rachel's a few doors down on High Street.

2011: No robins heard around the yard this morning. Rachel's ginkgo shedding, but - like all the others in town - still holds. The witch hazel leaves now are brown and brittle. The cold front of tomorrow and the next two days should bring them down. Many different types of bees and flies swarmed around the last late mum in bloom in this last warm day for a while.

Ed Oxley stopped as he drove by to work, said he had seen the first large flock of crows west of town, "hundreds of them," he added. By late this afternoon, Lil's maple is almost completely bare. Jerry and Lee's maple is down to maybe a fourth. The river birch is full gold, keeps most of its leaves. A few weak crickets tonight, and one slow katydid near Greg's old house.

2012: Robins still chirping in the alley, most of the silver maples coming down, autumn violets still blooming, all the asters gone in the woods, the late red mum with the gold center is still in full bloom along the north garden.

2013: The beech on Dayton Street has its full rusty color. A few roses, tousled by frost, brought in and put in a vase.

2014: Robins still moving in the high trees of the neighborhood, half a dozen or so at a time. Then to the Monastery of St. Clare to rake leaves. On the trip, I saw many small flocks of starlings flying back and forth from field to field, lining up, too, on the high wires. Bradford pears were full color throughout the trip: leaves shades of glossy red-orange, deep gold, flapping in the wind like aspens. Zinnias pulled up from the garden in the afternoon, dahlias dug and brought inside.

2017: To Ellis Pond, sun and a chilly wind: Dogwoods purple red, tulip trees golden brown, red oak and scarlet oak rusty brown, columnar oak brown and mostly shed, sawtooth oak dark brown and most leaves holding, pin oak golden saddle brown, cypress orange with some foliage half gone, silver maple curled and shedding, sycamore bare, willow wilted, sweet gum some green some red, most sugar maples gone but one at half bright orange gold, full American chestnut and sweetheart chestnut deep orange brown, Chinese maple red orange full, Zelcova shedding but most holding, still golden rust.

Along High Street, Lil's maple still full gold and about a fourth down, Mrs. Timberlake's maple over half down, Frank's silver maple with withered leaves coming down, Rachel's ginkgo olive green. Xenia Avenue ginkgoes solid dusky gold, very little leafdrop so far. In the fish food: five camel crickets, the most ever. And squirrels or raccoons are back in the attic banging and clumping around just before sunrise. Lamium blooming in the east garden. Rick said he heard a few tree frogs call in the night.

2018: Hard freeze near 27 last night. Many ginkgoes are starting to come down. When I checked the climbing bittersweet this morning, I saw that the bright orange berries had begun to emerge from their hulls; two days ago, I couldn't find any coming out.

2019: Hard freeze like last year. The white mulberry and the paulonia leaves have started to fall now, may be completely down by the end of the day. The last castor bean plant has finally given in to the cold, leaves tight against their branches, gnarled and crisp. At Jill's, all the silver maple leaves are down. Across the street, the canopy of Mrs. Timberlake's maple is collapsing. Afternoon: Jill called to say all the ginkgo leaves in town came down over night. And in my back yard, the white mulberry tree and the paulonia are bare. At Ellis Pond, at least a hundred geese in the field. Leslie reports five juncos at her Talus Drive location.

2020: A morning walk at 7:30, sun and mild: Robins all about, crows south of town, chattering of sparrows and wrens, a red-bellied woodpecker and a blue jay; a red-shouldered hawk as I walked home from Jill's house at 9:00. To Buck Creek State Park in the afternoon: the landscape color lingers in pear trees, beeches, the hardiest maples and sweet gums.

2021: A robin peeping in the honeysuckles this morning. At Ellis Pond (where I haven't been since Ranger died in March) seemed foreign to me this afternoon. No geese. Most leaves down, except in the oak grove, which was dusky golden-green. I felt disconnected from the leafturn sequence, lost in space and time.

2022: Robins common throughout the neighborhood, mild weather continuing in spite of the full moon and high barometer (30.75).

Journal

All my knowledge of the world, even my scientific knowledge, is gained from my own particular point of view, or from some experience of the world without which the symbols of science would be meaningless.

Maurice Merleau-Ponty

I have been watching the maple tree across the street from our house for about twenty-five years. I have notes about when it flowers in the spring and notes about when it loses all its leaves. It used to be Lil's maple; she died a while ago, but the tree has kept its name.

Except for a newly planted maple next door to it, Lil's sugar maple is always the latest on my block to lose its leaves. The earliest date it shed all its foliage was October 30 in 2004. There was a warm hard wind that day, temperature reaching into the upper 70s, and I planted lilies along the edge of the northeast garden.

In 1999, Lil's maple was down by October 31; even the pear leaves were falling early along Xenia Avenue that year. In 1988, the pivot date was November 4, the same day my white mulberry came undone. On November 6, 1990, a huge low-pressure system cut away the last ridge of Middle Fall, hurled the ginkgo leaves outside my window against the ground in 40-mile-per-hour gusts, and stripped Lil's stubborn maple bare. This year (as of today, November 8), that tree is holding late, the last fragments refusing to give up. Maybe they will last until the 15th, like in 1985 and 2007.

In the face of summer's collapse, I collect my observations to narrow the scope of change, nurturing myopia to defend the illusion of control. November is running away with everything, all the green and warmth are disappearing, but I contain the catastrophe, shrink it to size, with the tree across the street, watching hard, framing, measuring and pretending.

Grass withers; and the flowers too fade.
Seize the short joys then, ere they vade.

Andrew Marvel

A true November day, chill and wet. I walked in the sodden woods, looking for walnuts.... How good to sit by the fire on such a day as this, and how good to go out again in the wet.

Harlan Hubbard

Sunrise/set: 7:13/5:25
Day's Length: 10 hours 12 minutes
Average High/Low: 53/36
Average Temperature: 45
Record High: 79 – 1975, 78 – 2020
Record Low: 22 – 1957

The Daily Weather
On ten percent of the days, highs reach 70 degrees or above; on 20 percent they reach the 60s; on 35 percent they reach 50. Forties come one fourth of the time, with 30s ten percent of the time. Frost strikes 45 percent of the nights. The sun fails to appear about half the time, rain falls 55 percent of the years, snow just once in a quarter century. Today and tomorrow together often bring more precipitation than any other two days of the month.

The Natural Calendar
Along the Gulf of Mexico, the trees still hold their foliage, and colors haven't even reached their peak. By the time second spring is halted by snow and cold in Indiana, it will be reaching its fulfillment in Georgia. By the time the last leaves fall in the southern Appalachians during the middle of December, the first new leaves will be emerging in Florida. The last day of harvest in Ohio will be the first day of planting a thousand miles south where the last wildflower of one year will be blooming beside the first of the next.

Daybook
1983: Covered Bridge: Grass still grows, one dandelion in bloom, nettles new. Only yellowing Osage foliage is left. Seeds sprouting

in rotten logs, sweet smell of fallen leaves and autumn ground.

1984: After a rainy cool day, craneflies mating on the picnic table.

1985: Geese fly over at 5:06 p.m.

1987: Mock orange almost gone.

1988: Cardinal sings at 7:30 a.m. Some goldenrod on Corry Street still has color.

1989: The poplar outside my south window has come apart in this windy week. Lil's maple still has almost all its leaves. She's got the latest maple in town. The white mulberry (my guide, from my back door, for the position of the sun at summer solstice) is still green, but the forsythia bushes along the house are starting to thin out. I can see through to the street now.

1990: Geese fly over the yard at 8:00 a.m. The last ginkgoes fall at Wilberforce.

1991: Large flocks of blackbirds downtown Dayton, along the river, over the highway.

1992: White mulberry holds on in the back yard, small-flowered yellow mum in full bloom in the front garden.

1997: Forsythia thinning. My maple finally all comes down. Lil's maple starting to unravel. Leaves raked today, probably more than three fourths of the harvest. Cardinals singing this morning near 7:00, crows calling. Geese are all over the DeWine Pond shore.

1999: Four deer seen crossing Dayton-Yellow Springs Road at 6:30 this evening. I almost hit one of them on the way to tai chi; on the way back, I saw a dead doe by the side of the road. Rutting season.

2000: Crows at 6:58 a.m. Birch, magnolia and sweet gums three-fourths down. Skunk tonight, the third in recent nights.

2001: Phil calls: Buzzards are still gathering near sundown at the corner of President Street and Orton Road.

2002: A cardinal sang once at 6:52 a.m., then once more around 8:00. Leaves are yellowing quickly on the blue flag iris, the Stella d'oro lilies, and the hosta. Honeysuckle leaf-drop accelerating, quince almost all down. Danielson's maple is about seven-eighths fallen, my workshop-window maple is also almost down. The back Osage is still green. Comfrey is lush, two feet high, enjoying second spring.

2003: Almost all the white mulberry leaves are down now. The last red mulberry tree is bare as well. Grackles heard in the back trees this morning. Starlings fill the wires along the roads to Dayton.

2005: Most honeysuckles are down now, red berries prominent. Rose of Sharon fell this week. Most leaves of the pink quince dropped today.

2006: Mild in the 60s today. A cardinal sang at 6:53 this morning, and saw a bright yellow sulphur butterfly outside of Wilmington. Two deer stood in my way as I drove to work along Grinnell Road, one a fat buck. Downtown, the decorative pear trees have their full colors, red and gold and rusty brown; shedding is underway. In the greenhouse, some of the Christmas cacti have begun to fade – especially the red plant.

2007: Mateo's black walnut tree has lost all but one walnut. The Limestone Street tree keeps just a handful. Mateo's red mulberry foliage is yellow green now, Lil's maple full color, Danielsons' darker and shedding, Mrs. Timberlake's full, and the magnolia next door to her is mottled and thinning. The Korean lilac is pale and about two-thirds down.

2008: More and more leaves down: All the serviceberry, all the red mulberry, the hackberry and the elms. The large spirea in the alley has lost almost all its golden brown foliage. Redbuds are falling, mock orange weakening. Lil's maple is three-fourths gone, all the others completely bare. The beech on Dayton Street is half burnt sienna. The quince leaves, yellow-green, are dropping into the pond.

2009: A warm 52 degrees this morning and a bright red sky. Mrs. Timberlake's silver maple and Frank's are more than half down. The Dayton Street beech is more than three-fourths fallen, and all the pear trees downtown are red orange.

2010: Fruit falling from the decorative pear tree on Stafford Street. Robins peeping throughout the neighborhood. Sparrows chattering, distant starlings and crows. The Dayton Street beech is half rusty gold, half golden green. Sweet gums continue to shed; most sycamore leaves have shriveled. In the greenhouse, the old Christmas cacti have put out a few flowers.

2011: The Dayton Street Beech has started to shed. No robins this morning. All the silver maples in the neighborhood are down. Lil's maple is bare, as is her burning bush - red berries taking the place of leaves.

2013: To Cincinnati: Bright sun, mild south wind: Many maples still in place, but burnished pear leaves become prominent now in the thinning roadsides. Three large flocks of starlings seen, one mixed with crows feeding in a soybean field. Frank's silver maple is down. The quince continues to pace Lil's maple at about three-fourths shed. At Ellis, late afternoon, the scarlet oak was a rich red-brown, the sugar maples had lost their foliage, the hickory bare. The leaves of the Siberian elms and the remaining leaves of the tulip trees and sycamores were twisted from the frost. Neysa and I walked with Bella along the blue water's edge, seven buzzards sailing in the gusts above us.

2014: Robins still calling back and forth in the mornings. Small flocks of starlings common. At Ellis Pond, the cypress needles are starting to shed. Most of the oaks have brown, brittle leaves, except for the scarlet oak, which is deep scarlet, and the sawtooth oak, the leaves of which are still mostly green and whole. The silver maples are palomino gold, as usual, and the Siberian elms are thinning. In the alley, bright orange fruits emerging from a few white euonymus berries, and all the bittersweet vines are full of bright orange berries, leaves all withered around them. I removed the net from above the pond this afternoon, most of the quince and other leaves already down.

2015: Most ginkgoes still hold at half. The back yard is still dominated by the deep gold of the white mulberry, the two Osage and Jeanie's redbud. In the greenhouse, the geraniums have started to recover from the intense summer weather, and the Christmas cacti are fully budded, ready to bloom any day.

2016: At Ellis Pond, more than a hundred Canadian geese congregating along the shore, entering the water one by one. Sycamores are about gone there, and the cypress foliage has thinned considerably. Throughout town, the peak is well past, and the streets are ragged and disheveled. Zelcovas are bare at the top, rusty orange below. Many pears are burnished. Lil's maple stands out on High Street, keeping its color even as its leaves fall. In the yard, the river birch and the redbuds are orange-gold, and half down; the trumpet creeper vine on the south end of the porch is a weak light green. The pink quince near the pond still holds most of its leaves, although it has finally started to give in to the colder nights. On the north side of the house, the some vines of the euonymus that had taken over the siding are blanching, and white berries prominent. Walking downtown, Jill noticed a single purple iris in bloom across from the grade school.

2017: Deep cold settling in for the first time this autumn. Jeanie's river birch began to shed more heavily overnight, the ground spreading from the trunk sheathed with gold. The last castor bean plants killed by frost this morning, the north-side viburnum finally dropping almost all its remaining leaves. At the shop and post office, Kentucky coffee trees bare with its dirt brown seeds all lined up on its branches, Zelcovas rusty brown and all intact, pears just starting.

2018: Light snow in the night. This morning, Jill called to report the foliage of the large gingkoes at the south end of town was shedding quickly, coverlets of gold under them all. Rachel's ginkgo still holds. Robins peeping in the neighborhood around 8:00 a.m. The last castor bean plant was killed yesterday morning, and the year settles in to its Late Fall character.

2019: To Cincinnati and back: Leaves are down throughout the area. Several murmurations of starlings seen. At Ellis Pond, the goose population is growing, maybe several hundred now – the most since Late Winter. The cypress foliage strips easily from its branches. The weeping willows are ragged and worn.

2020: Moya's tulip tree and my red viburnum are just about gone, Lil's maple down to maybe a fourth of its leaves. Rachel's ginkgo has fallen.

2021: Lil's tree and Mrs. Timberlake's tree hold along High Street, Lil's especially rich, shown off by the full scarlet of the burning bush and Japanese maple beside it. Robins again heard peeping in the honeysuckles this morning as I dug canna lily bulbs and was getting the ground ready for transplanting New England asters, a few hybrid willows for the west end of the property, and the first of the new phlox. (My gardening notes here one more way of keeping track...for years from now, when the plantings have taken over the yard or have disappeared or have been replaced.)

2022: The white mulberry is down now, but the Osage still holds at half. Jill reports sixty geese at the Antioch pond at the west end of town. Paul left a message saying he had seen a bald eagle on the lone dead tree beyond Ellis as well as above the Unitarian Fellowship building south of town.

Our northern November day itself is like spring water. It is melted frost, dissolved snow. There is a chill in it and an exhilaration also. The forenoon is all morning and the afternoon all evening. The shadows seem to come forth and to revenge themselves upon the day. The sunlight is diluted with darkness. The colors fade from the landscape, and only the sheen of the river lights up the gray and brown distance.
John Burroughs

November 10th
The 314th Day of the Year

The field
Strewn with its dank yellow drifts
Of withered leaves, and the elms,
Fades into dimness apace.

Matthew Arnold

Sunrise/set: 7:14/5:24
Day's Length: 10 hours 10 minutes
Average High/Low: 53/35
Average Temperature: 44
Record High: 70 – 1975, 78 – 2020
Record Low: 19 – 1957

The Daily Weather

High temperatures reach above 70 on five percent of the afternoons, are in the 60s on 15 percent of the afternoons, the 50s on 40 percent, 40s on 35 percent, 30s on five percent. Rain comes four days in ten, snow one in ten. The sun shines 60 percent of the years. Morning lows drop below freezing almost half the time.

The Natural Calendar

Landmark trees that are especially prominent or familiar measure the end of fall better than almost any other gauge. Along the 40th Parallel, ginkgoes are excellent markers for the end of October and the beginning of November. The white mulberries are a little later, and they are equally dramatic in the way they suddenly collapse. Silver maples, oaks, sweet gums, Osage, and beeches can persist well into November, and the decorative pears into the first part of December. A world away on Australia's Christmas Island, millions of red crabs begin their migration to the sea.

Daybook

1982: Water striders on the river this afternoon. Squirrels chasing each other in a sycamore. Cricket heard at the covered bridge.

89

1983: Ginkgo leaves collapsed all at once down into a golden coverlet around the trunk.

1985: Geese flew over at 8:16 a.m. This afternoon I went out past the covered bridge in the rain, up the west ridge above the river. The water was high and running fast, the main branch was muddy, leaves tumbling in the current, tips emerging like feeding fish. Honeysuckle leaves were a tawny green beside me. The pink leaves of a dogwood were shining through the wet undergrowth, as exotic as the dogwood flowers of April. My feelings can't distinguish the decaying leaves from the spring blossoms. That's the illusion of second spring, the emotional misreading of the remaining colors, choosing to interpret them as signs of rebirth instead of the last fragments of the summer's whole.

1986: Geese fly over at 8:30 and 9:25 a.m. My ginkgo is gone in a pile of bright gold. Some pear foliage downtown has patches of reddish brown.

1988: Almost all the last leaves disappear in a thunderstorm, an inch of rain, winds past 35 miles an hour. Pussy willow, apple, cherry, my poplar blown clean. All but the oaks and willows in the countryside are down. One Osage in the back holds. At Sycamore Hole, the river is as high as I've ever seen it, no hint of the early summer's drought.

1990: Large flock of geese goes over at eight o'clock this morning.

1993: Cardinals still singing off and on in the mornings. Dozens of robins at the entry to South Glen, still migrating. One dandelion seen today at Wilberforce, a few aster flowers.

1997: Lil's maple has lost about half its leaves. Silver olives are three-fourths gone along the freeway. Honeysuckles down to a fourth. Witch hazel full bloom. Many maples still full color now. When I stood in the back yard this morning before sunrise, the streetlight was shining in my eye for the first time since May.

2001: Many of the remaining leaves on Lil's maple have shriveled and lost their color without falling, the first time I ever remember that happening. Usually her tree comes down with leaves still soft and pure yellow.

To Jacoby in the late afternoon with Bella, our border collie pup, temperature mild, the sky streaked with high cirrus, the sun low and almost white, the woods floor bright with chickweed, moneywort, buttercup, mint, henbit, garlic mustard, waterleaf and leafcup. Wind in the high trees sometimes shutting out the sounds of the highway to the west. Two tan moths. The call of one flicker or pileated woodpecker. Tattered seed tufts on the asters and white snakeroot. I came across a dead vole, sleek and fat, curled on the moss on top of a stone by the path. He looked as if he were sleeping, having found the perfect bed, oblivious to the daylight and to our presence.

At the swamp, below the stark, dead trees, new dark green ragwort, dock, purple skunk cabbage, fresh water cress filling the clear rivulets. Bella and I walked across the spongy surface of the marsh on clumps of crisp grass and lanky thistles, between the foliage of the April iris, the old stalks of ironweed, disheveled cattails, and the sprawling remnants of angelica.

I remembered wild ginger here in April, cowslip and toad trillium in full bloom, buckeyes leafing out, first garlic mustard flowering, first phlox, toothwort and spring beauties in patches, wild iris up and budding, ferns unraveling, purple and yellow and white violets everywhere

Uncovered by the disappearance of the canopy, time was so clear and distinct across Jacoby. The absence of the flowers seemed more illusion than truth. The swamp was like the firmament, and its particles were earthstars that revolved around my memory and contained the soul of all those other seasons which preceded and which will follow this season.

At home, one cricket heard again tonight.

2002: One cardinal singing on High Street: 6:58 to 7:06 a.m.

2004: Robins passing through this morning. The white mulberry is shedding in a different way this year, leaves coming down slowly over a period of the past week – instead of all at once.

2005: White mulberries are holding in most areas. The ginkgo is half down by my window at school, the other two have shed completely. The ginkgo on Xenia Avenue near the south end of Yellow Springs is full gold. Poplars are almost all bare between here and Wilmington. Many gum trees have collapsed. Oaks are red-brown and holding, beeches rusty brown. Hosta leaves have decayed quickly over the past week. Starlings clucking along Dayton Street at 7:45 this morning.

2006: The beech tree on Dayton Street is more than half down, and the pear trees on Xenia Avenue are shedding all at once.

2007: A cardinal was singing when I came out to start the car this morning about 7:45. In the alley, the very last of the walnuts from Mateo's black walnut tree came down overnight. The Limestone black walnut tree has about a dozen left. Lil's maple is deep orange-gold today and starting to shed. To Sharonville near Cincinnati: More than half of the leaves are down, but many bright colors remain from oaks, sweet gum, sycamore, ginkgo, silver and sugar maples, smoke bush, crab apple, pear, even ash and cottonwood in this late year. Large flocks of starlings on telephone wires seen throughout the drive. One cabbage butterfly seen in the north garden late this afternoon.

2008: One petal left on Frank's red rose. In the alley, the euonymus berries are turning pink, but not opening. Don's burning bush is almost completely down.

2009: Ginkgo shedding along Dayton street. Frank's and Mrs. Timberlake's silver maples are almost all down.

2010: Across the countryside, honeysuckle foliage is still prominent, yellow-green.

2011: Kit called to report a huge flock of blackbirds on the way to Beavercreek. "One field was black with them," she said.

2012: I planted Jeanie's Turk's-Cap lilies in the late afternoon sun, and then one hundred blue hyacinths for May. Jeanie's river birch has turned gold now, shedding just a little. All the New England aster leaves are yellowing. On the way to Cincinnati, I noticed the silver maples holding palomino gold, and the pears ruddy. When Bella and I walked in the night, I smelled a skunk anticipating spring along High Street.

2013: Wind almost 20 miles an hour this morning, crows at 7:09.

2014: Deep cold system dropping down from Canada, connected to a Pacific typhoon, has brought over a foot of snow to Minneapolis and is due to strike deep into the South. But here today, there was sun and a high near 60. I walked in the woods with Bella without a jacket. Judy reports large flocks of starlings throughout her drive to Indianapolis two days ago. Osage foliage in the backyard is still intact and green. Jeanie's river birch full ochre, still keeping most of its leaves. New England aster leaves yellowing.

2016: This evening at the junction of Clifton Gorge and John Bryan Park, high above the river, Jill and I saw a handful of robins far to the west moving through the upper canopy, a fragment, perhaps of a migrating flock.

2017: After a low of 24 last night, sugar maples, silver maples and white mulberry leaves clatter down together, almost all down by afternoon. Mrs. Timberlake's and Frank's maples, the paulownia, the old peach and Jeanie's river birch collapsed in the dark. High Street lawns filling with leaves. Amy sends a photo of ginkgoes coming undone. When I went to add birdseed to the feeders, I surprised a young squirrel, maybe a third or half grown climbing the feeder pole. It froze and then jumped and raced to the back porch. When I left the house in the afternoon, I noticed Rachel's ginkgo was down (olive green at 8:00 a.m.). North to Delaware, Ohio, all the ginkgoes have come down across the area.

2018: Almost exactly like last year on this date: hard freeze in the lower 20s, silver maples and burning bush foliage down (Lil's and many others), Rachel's ginkgo with a skirt of gold, the back white mulberry leaves clattering to the ground. With almost all the red and gold maples fallen, the Dayton Street beech and Peggy's pear tree stand against the cold.

2019: The air has softened as the barometer slides toward a storm due tomorrow. In the honeysuckles of the neighborhood, I heard robins peeping this morning. Across the street, Lil's Norway maple keeps its leaves, ochre-gold, and her burning bush holds strong, while all around it, the maples are bare. Geese flew over at 9:52 as I was writing this update. This afternoon, several hundred geese seen in the fields across from Ellis Pond, and a small contingent on the water. Casey called to say he had seen red-winged blackbirds flying with a murmuration of starlings. Were the red-wings planning to stay the winter?

2020: A last warm day, upper 50s at dawn, chattering of robins, sparrows, cardinals (many "chit" calls), wrens, crows, blue jays, loud rattle of the tree crickets. In the field beyond Ellis, grass hoppers are still common.

2021: Heavy fog this morning encloses the faltering trees, grays the golds. In the night, many blossoms of the white Christmas cactus have opened in the greenhouse, and the remaining reds are all suddenly budded. Jill reports Asian lady beetles in her upstairs bathroom. Along Dayton Street, the beech tree is rusty gold. On High Street, Moya's tulip tree is darkening to a glowing brown, and Lil's tree is deep yellow, speckled with decay. The Danielsons' maple is bare, as is Frank's maple. Mrs. Timberlake's is half down. At the Glass Farm pond, the half-dozen ducks keep watch over the great blue heron on its log. Fifteen phlox plants put in behind the New England asters this afternoon, and then two dozen or so daffodils around them.

2022: Lil's leaves have been shriveled and dark for over a week; I note my surprise at that in 2001. Leah reports a sulphur butterfly in her garden this last warm day of the month. Hurricane Nicole comes ashore in eastern Florida, causing considerable harm, and now heads up the Southeast, due to bring rain tonight and tomorrow to Ohio.

2023: Jill reports numerous small murmurations of starlings along the fields south of town. And patches of bright color still. Around town, many burning bush leaves remain, and my gangly hydrangea near the crabapple tree keeps its pale yellow-beige leaves. News reports say that the globe has not been this warm in 125,000 years: so far not noticeable in Yellow Springs.

White as meal the frosty field,
Warm the fireside haven.
Not to autumn will I yield;
Not to winter even.

Robert Louis Stevenson

November 11th
The 315th Day of the Year

Leaves are falling from their branches,
All their power gone.
Trees are pale and bare.
Streams run high through the empty fields.
Frost burns the last, soft sprouts.
Birds huddle in these shortest days
and mourn the chill of the sky:
Our golden sun is fleeing into Sagittarius,
Leaving days of snow and nights of ice.

Manuscript of Benedictbeurn, *De ramis cadunt folia*

Sunrise/set: 7:15/5:23
Day's Length: 10 hours 8 minutes
Average High/Low: 52/35
Average Temperature: 44
Record High: 75 – 1902, est. 78 - 2020
Record Low: 20 – 1980

The Daily Weather

Today's high temperature distribution: 70s five percent, 60s ten percent, 50s thirty percent, 40s twenty percent, 30s thirty-five percent. A dramatic increase in the number of freezing predawn temperatures starts today, the lows below 32 growing from a frequency average of 40 percent up to 70 percent. Rain occurs 25 percent of the years, snow 15 percent.

The Natural Calendar

In a collage of different years, the second week of November in Yellow Springs, mixes storms and frost, butterflies and the seemingly fickle times of leaf fall from one tree and season to the next.

The day's length, refocused from the change from Daylight Saving Time, pulls back the progress of the year to the sunrise time of late February and the first days of Early Spring, but now the sun goes down almost as late as it does in Deep Winter.

Some years, the tallest maples and the ginkgo trees are bare by Armistice Day. Sometimes they are full gold. White mulberry trees can remain green or lose their foliage in a day. Some years, the pear trees that used to grace the downtown were ruddy and shedding, other years they kept the village in summer.

Grackles and starlings sometimes visit Bill Duncan Park, sometimes cross the sky from northeast to southwest in long files. Some years the robins are still plentiful in the honeysuckles. Sometimes they are gone by now. Canadian geese are restless, sometimes gather in sizeable numbers in the fields near Ellis Pond. Usually, male goldfinches have lost their gold by the first week of November. This year, I watched a goldfinch feeding, still half-summer color like my mulberry tree.

Some years on warm evenings, a few crickets still sing. In the milder afternoons, cabbage white butterflies come out to look for the last flowers. Two years ago this week, I even saw a monarch butterfly sail across the yard. Twenty years ago this week, I found a grass snake lying in the sun near the old dam past the mill. One year we had the first snow and then deep frost this week.

Even in the varied events of Late Fall's arrival this week, the point-counterpoint of warmth and cold, the differences in the times and quality of peak leaf color, seen against the same week through the decades, have their own characters. In human history, the close of the Great War in 1918 is only one of an endless number of events to be woven into the fabric of memory. Even as the climate changes, natural history still repeats itself enough to form a separate space for these days within the local year, a place in which the greater anomalies are only part of the counterpoint.

Daybook

1983: The white mulberry in the back yard is coming down quickly now. A few Queen Anne's lace still in bloom along Wilberforce-Clifton Road.

1984: The white mulberry begins to lose its leaves, but they are still mostly green. First snow. First snowball made. Kale and chard thriving in the changeable weather, one-day frost, then rain, then a day in the 70s. The grass still growing.

1985: How many notes and observations are enough? There are never enough.

1986: From my east window, I see the ginkgo leaves all came down last night with the first snow. The white mulberry dropped all its leaves overnight, too. Bradford pears trees uptown are more stubborn; they darken slowly, browning and stiffening.

1990: Geese flew over about 8:00 this morning. Almost all leaves down along the freeway, but one willow was green.

1991: Upper Grinnell: Honeysuckle is still a barrier in places. Miterwort foliage is strong. High sun on the treetops at sundown. The silver winding river, the fallen logs invisible in summer, lie below me in the bare valley.

1992: Many sweet gum trees are still red orange in town, have most of their leaves. The south lilac is green and full. It is still Middle Fall in the Osage woods.

1993: At South Glen, dozens of robins just inside the preserve at the bridge. They seem to be heading south along the tree line. I found them here a week or so ago, too. Were they separated from a main flock? Will they spend the winter? One dandelion blossom seen, milkweed pods coming completely undone, seeds adrift. Only occasional asters in very late bloom here and there, maybe one or two pale flowers to a plant.

1999: In this mildest November, the white mulberry holds at half. A few ginkgoes on High Street have kept half their leaves, too.

2001: South Glen: a dozen turkey vultures circling low over the butterfly preserve.

2002: Cardinals sing at 6:53 this morning, continue on and off for an hour or so. The sun came up over the south corner of the Danielson's house (as seen from my bedroom window). Tornadoes in Van Wert, a hundred miles north, last night. The hostas here collapsed in the overnight inch-and-a-half rain. My shed window maple leaves came down, too. More than half the honeysuckles are gone. Most of the redbuds have lost their foliage, maybe three dozen leaves hold on our tree in the north yard. Lil's maple has about a third of its leaves. Stella d'oro lilies still have buds. The beech on Dayton Street is full copper-orange. The yearling peach still has all its leaves, but the parent tree beside it has been bare for weeks. Robins whinnying in the back lot.

2006: In the yard, I found seed heads everywhere, spent rose petals, rose hips I should have cut back a month ago, dried hydrangea blossoms covered in spider webs, Joe Pye weed bushy and dun like burdock, three blue spiderworts out of season, hops heavy across the honeysuckles, oodles of black redbud seeds hanging like manes in the branches, the soft green seeds of the fierce wood nettle, red crab apples bigger than I'd ever noticed before, stiff and prickly burrs of purple coneflowers.

Everything around me seemed benign and soothing: a handful of soft, dark red raspberries from the patch that failed to produce much of anything this year, crabgrass gone to seed, its claws not threatening but protective, the summer mallow crumbling away, a skipper and a naked lady butterfly and a cabbage white ruffled by the breeze in the zinnias, honeybees climbing in the asters, and the chirping and chirping of sparrows north of the garden.

As I walked, the wind picked up, pushing fat cumulus clouds so fast, and I felt surrounded and safe within an enclosure of motion and sound. All of a sudden the air was cold and clouds moved over me, and the afternoon turned cruel and hollow. Then just as quickly there was sun again, and I felt at home and at peace.

2007: Gray and rainy today, the High Street maples are shedding: the Danielsons' the most, then Lil's, then Mrs. Timberlake's. In the alley, one dandelion, one purslane, a few violet aster plants three or four inches tall with flowers, one goldenrod stalk bright gold in Don's garden, one yellow stella d'oro, too. We've had many light frosts but no hard frost yet; the elephant ears are bedraggled and singed, but some are still tall and healthy. Most of the tree of heaven foliage stays, as well, burned but remaining attached to the branches. The white mulberry tree and Rachel's ginkgo are completely green, and many of our redbuds keep their red-green leaves. Moya's maple and the secret maple both came down about four days ago.

2008: The white mulberry leaves began to break off this morning at dawn. Then they fell through the morning, all down by the time I went out to the woodpile after lunch. On High Street a ways, the Osage tree lost most of its leaves within a few hours. Our Osage remains impassive.

2009: Mrs. Timberlake's silver maple is almost all down, as is Frank's. Starlings chattering to the north. The ginkgo on Dayton Street is coming down quickly, more than three-fourths shed, and the white mulberry in the back yard had lost at least half its leaves by this morning, after a hard wind all night. Ruby called about 11:00 o'clock, wished me happy 11/11 at 11. She told me the story of her Armistice Day of 91 years ago in Yosemite, Kentucky. Her family's party-line phone rang (five short rings for her house) at 11:00 p.m. The news was that the armistice had been signed. All the women in the town, Ruby said, grabbed a rolling pin and started beating on pans or whatever. The men "shot off anvils" – placing dynamite in the hole of one anvil, setting another anvil on top of that, and then setting it off with a black-powder fuse. "You could hear that around the world," she said.

2010: Crows heard at 7:01, starlings singing on the east side of Stafford Street at 10:00, occasional robins, many sparrows chattering, the weather cool and clear. In the alley, Mrs. Timberlake's silver maple and Frank's silver maple still hold pale green and gold, leaves contracting now. This afternoon I cut the grass for the last time, the temperature in the middle 60s, sky clear and the air still. From Springfield, Missouri, Jeffery Goss, Jr. writes: "First juncos and starlings of the season."

2011: A sizeable flock of starlings this morning around 10:00 along Stafford Street. The New England aster and the goldenrod foliage is turning violet-ochre. The oak-leaf hydrangeas are purple-red. The Annabelle hydrangea is a pale yellow. Today, the river birch in the backyard lost all its leaves. Rachel's ginkgo is down, but the Dayton Street ginkgo is still holding at full color. The downtown pears have turned and have shed about half their leaves, and the Dayton Street beech is two-thirds gone, our white mulberry and Osage still strong.

2012: The scarlet oaks at Ellis Pond have shed most of their leaves, and the sawtooth oak is ochre now and starting to lose its foliage. It will be the last tree to come down. The swamp chestnut oak, though, is holding its dried, shriveled, brittle leaves: how long will they stay? At home, deeper turning of the New England aster leaves, and Jeanie's river birch has turned to a pale full gold. The day was mild in the 70s with a strong breeze, and I planted the last of the spring bulbs in the circle garden, in the front garden and around the birch and cherry trees: one hundred aconites, five golden crocus and nine early spring orange tulips. In the warm sun, honey bees and bee flies and bumble bees swarmed around the blooms of the last red-orange mum.

2014: The Dayton Street birch is full orange-gold-green, at least half gone. Three buzzards were circling the village, and a medium-sized flock of starlings passed over High Street when I was walking Bella around 9:00 this morning.

2015: Two of the Xenia Avenue ginkgoes still hold most of their leaves; Rachel's ginkgo is half down, others in town ragged. Robins still peeping in the morning. Great mare's tails in the sky all day, the wind picking up in the late afternoon, storms and hard wind forecast for tonight (snow across the southern Plains). As I went to the gym, I looked up and saw two dozen vultures circling but also seeming to move toward the southwest. Many dandelions and a few violets blooming in the Antioch lawn. At home, two small, yellow reblooming lily blossoms are nodding below the ripe bittersweet. I set in the last of almost four hundred bulbs before dark, twenty large yellow crocus in the dooryard and twenty-four aconites at the west end of the fishpond.

2017: To Cincinnati and back, hard freeze at 22 degrees: One large flock of starlings or blackbirds, several small murmurations of starlings. Morning mare's tails turned to gray altostratus by noon.

There was no frost on the car window yesterday morning, even though it was sunny through until night, and no frost this morning: the warm front gave a two-day warning. Rain tomorrow.

2018: The white mulberry has shed its leaves throughout the day, almost all of them gone by dark. In the countryside, only the deep maroon oaks, some mottled sycamores and sweet gums and occasional Norway maples hold along the tree lines. Ed Oxley told me that thousands of crows have started to gather north of town in the fields along East Enon Road.

2020: I woke up to find the white mulberry tree in the backyard had lost about half its remaining leaves in the night. In the dark east, the crescent moon was holding bright Venus in its cup.

With last night's rain, Lil's maple and burning bush, Moya's tulip tree, Peggy's pear tree, Jill's Japanese maple, most of the yard's honeysuckles and the Dayton Street beech had fallen. The cypress trees were bare, oak grove thinning at the pond.

It was the last warm day, upper 50s at dawn, record high near 80 for the afternoon, chattering of robins, sparrows, cardinals (many "chit" calls), wrens, crows, blue jays, slurred rattle of the tree crickets. In the field beyond Ellis, grass hoppers were still common.

I checked my barometer, and I was pulled along into another of my vigils for winter, waiting at the top of a barometric cliff that would unbalance the heat wave of Late Autumn's Summer and plunge it into rain and cold.

I could not see beyond my yard. I was closed in by the remaining foliage, walls of sundry golds, from lemon-yellow mulberry, to mango shades of lily spears, decorative grasses transfixed by the low sun, beige honeysuckle, mustard shades of small aster and New England aster leaves (their flowers all tufted now), yellow-green English elm, glowing winterberry clusters, apricot shades of redbud, chartreuse Osage, amber bittersweet, earth and sky confused, in which fallen leaves were the same colors and textures as those left on the trees, and it was hard for me to tell if the sparrows feeding among them were the wind or birds, and the barometer kept dropping, more warmth in its wake, the atmospheric ritual before the frost of the week ahead, the golden sun fleeing into Sagittarius.

2021: Wind in the morning, late maple leaves swirling in the streets as I drove to work. Leah came into the store in the afternoon to tell me she had all kinds of lady bugs in her house this week, yellow, red and green, she said, some with seven spots, some with 12. Jill had them yesterday: the return of the lady beetles after what seems like many years - the early decade of the century bringing the most sightings.

2023: When I went outside at 7:00 this morning, birds were twittering, but I couldn't tell if they there wrens or cardinals or robins; they sounded like a combination of all. three. At the monastery in Cincinnati, about all the trees were down. Flocks of birds noticed overhead. In town, zelcovas keep their rusty color and density, much stronger than the rawness of the woodlots, In the greenhouse, two Christmas cacti are blooming now, and three canna stalks have bright red blossoms And the tropical plumeria trees have held their leaves. Dimitra, the dancer, died this afternoon, and I thought of her and felt her happy in the freedom of this thin time and the open sky and landscape,.

All things that breathe and move with toil and sound
Are born and die; revolve, subside and swell.

Percy Bysshe Shelley

November 12th
The 316th Day of the Year

Beauty has no set weather, no sure place'
Her careful pageantries are here as there,
With nothing lost.

Lizette Woodworth Reese

Sunrise/set: 7:16/5:22
Day's Length: 10 hours 6 minutes
Average High/Low: 52/35
Average Temperature: 43
Record High: 71 – 1964
Record Low: 15 – 1911

The Daily Weather

Today's high temperatures: 60s twenty percent of the time, 50s thirty percent, 40s thirty percent, 30s twenty percent. Frost occurs about three mornings in four. Rain falls 35 percent of the time, snow five percent. Skies are clear to partly cloudy seven days in a decade.

The Natural Calendar

He comes, -- comes, -- The Frost Spirit comes!
let us meet him as we may,
And turn with the light of the parlor-fire
his evil power away....

John Greenleaf Whittier

At average elevations along the 40th Parallel, the second week of November is the first week of Late Fall, a time when most of the remaining leaves come down and the contours of the landscape become clear. Across the fields and hillsides, Grazing Season draws to a close as the pasture growth slows in the cold. Thinning Season beginning for Mock Orange and Forsythia, their steady leafdrop measuring the approach of frost.

The Season of Winter Clouds arrives from the west as the

average percentage of cloud cover doubles over summer and middle autumn's average. This week brings the Season of Tufted Gray Goldenrod and Thimbleweed Seeding Season. Deer Mating Season in the woods coincides with Witch Hazel Blooming Season in town and the Season of Red Berries throughout the parks as dogwoods, hawthorns, bayberry and flowering crabs reveal their color.

Summer's Hercules sets in the west by 10:00 p.m., and the Great Square of autumn moves in behind it. Cassiopeia lies due south of Polaris, its deepest intrusion overhead. Procyon of Canis Major is just emerging from the east.

Daybook

1982: Along King Street, all the Osage leaves are down. The hedgerows are bare, even the wild raspberry leaves gone. The honeysuckle holds, but it is weak and yellow. Forsythia is thinning. With the canopy gone, the sky has opened up above the river. With the sun shining, the water hasn't seemed so blue since the first day of May.

1983: Osage leaves still hold at half this morning, many maples too, a Dayton Street ginkgo half, the backyard white mulberry half (then most fell late this afternoon), most of the poplars hanging on and green. Pecan leaves withered. Some lilac leaves burned, but stay.

1986: Cardinal sings at 7:02 this morning, then again at 7:30.

1988: Chickweed thick and green in the bare purple raspberry canes.

1990: Geese at 7:45 this morning, a robin heard later. Bright sun and mid 40s. At the Covered Bridge taking pictures: sky a cloudless blue reflected in the river. The brightest November greens in the waterleaf and moss and glade grasses, then the yellow green of the honeysuckles. The woods quiet except for one cricket past the skunk cabbage patch. Downtown, sparrows were chattering in the red pear trees. Two dandelions were blooming at the corner of Clifton and Grinnell Roads. In the garden, chard has withered from frost, lettuce still all right, kale thriving, mums almost gone.

1992: Crickets steady and loud, their vibrating song in the southwest corner of the greenhouse. They chant from late afternoon through the morning. All-day rain today, turning to a storm by late afternoon; moaning of the wind fills the house. All the white mulberry leaves had come down by the time I got home from work.

1993: At the porch light this humid and warm morning, there were craneflies spinning. Behind the back trees, sporadic cardinal song, the young males trying out their mating songs as they mature before the winter sets in.

1995: Walking our bulldog, Buttercup, this morning: Two small flocks of crows were gathering, one to the east around the Catholic church, one to the north past Kingsfield

1999: The white mulberry still holds at half. Below it, the yellow leaves of the gooseneck plant match its color. In the pond, the koi are still active. Six leaves on the water lily; one red bud has been there quite a while waiting for more sun and warmth. Zinnias were killed in the last frost, but the snapdragons continue to bud and bloom. Along the expressways, honeysuckles and willows stay yellow green. Starlings and crows are flocking. Just outside of town, crows again in the soybean fields, maybe a hundred or so.

2003: The first jade tree flowers opened in the greenhouse this morning. Out in the countryside, the woodlots are bare; the past week took almost all their leaves. After a day in the 60s, barometer dropping, the wind picks up, blows hard through the evening, buffeting the truck as I drive home from Wilmington.

2005: The first red Christmas cactus flower opened last night in the greenhouse. Jerry and Lee's sweet gum tree is full yellow. One cabbage butterfly seen flying over the back porch this mild afternoon of sun and highs in the upper 60s.

2006: More than half of the Christmas cacti are done blooming now. In the garden, the tufted virgin's bower has chocolate brown leaves. The hostas have melted to slush; the New England aster leaves are gold and falling. In the countryside, banks of yellowing honeysuckles appear to be banks of April forsythia. At the south side of Mateo's property, the privet leaves are gone, blue berries prominent. At the corner of High and Limestone streets, bittersweet hulls cover the sidewalk. This morning at 7:00, a wren chattered along the north garden.

2008: In the alley, the small, golden maple yearlings are losing leaves now. The euonymus berries are getting redder, and a few more have opened. Bittersweet is showing more intensely now.

2010: Sparrows and chickadees fed heavily today, the sky clear and the temperature close to 70. I planted fifty red tulips by the circle garden just before sunset. Along Dayton Street, the great beech is burnished orange and gold. Orange winterberry seeds are emerging from their white hulls along the north garden wall. Honeysuckle and New England aster leaves are tinted dusky mauve.

2011: To St. Clare monastery and back this morning, sun coming up as I drove out around 7:20. A mild and brilliant day, high cirrus by afternoon. All the leaves are gone along the highway except the pears and honeysuckles and an occasional Osage, oak and silver maple. One small flock of starlings seen. At home, I noticed that the pachysandra plants were deep green and budded for spring. I swept honeysuckle berries from the front walk this afternoon. They are as much of a nuisance as red mulberries. The last quince leaves down; I raked them from the pond.

2012: Walked with Jeff at the Covered Bridge this afternoon. It had rained hard through the morning, and the river was as full as I've seen it this fall. The cold front had settled in, and the air was still. The honeysuckle leaves were glowing against the gray sky, and all the pastures were bright, bright green. Near the bridge, the goldenrod field was a solid, rich red-orange, leaves and spent flowers and stems all the same color, stiff in the freezing air. Far along the path, we came upon a flock of Eastern bluebirds moving south.

2013: Light snow and low 20s overnight, and as dawn came on, all the white mulberry leaves in the neighborhood fell down green, and all the bright yellow ginkgoes collapsed throughout town. The Dayton Street beech has lost half its foliage. To Wilmington and back: now only the hardiest maples, beeches, oaks and Osage hold on, most of the woods dark.

2014: In the greenhouse, red and white and pink Christmas cacti in early full bloom. Poinsettias noticed at the supermarket.

2015: In the greenhouse, the first white and red Christmas cactus blossomed, and the leaves of the white mulberry tree all came down in the hard wind. The Osage, however, has held on, and the small-leafed Chinese elm is still green and has not begun to shed. Downtown, the Zelcovas are coming apart. The koi were still feeding today, the water temperature remaining just above 50 degrees. Through the night, the wind was moaning.

2016: The first killing frost occurred this morning, withering all the zinnias and most of the castor beans. Lil's maple and burning bush shedding heavily. The Christmas cacti are fully budded, but not blooming yet. Many large murmurations of starlings seen in my round-trip to the St. Clare monastery in Cincinnati. At home, the Paulownia tree lost all its leaves in the frost, and Rachel's ginkgo is about a third down.

2017: Sizeable flock of starlings in the south garden trees at dawn. Pleasant early morning, then gray and raw with light rain in the afternoon and evening.

2018: The first morning in the teens, and the white mulberry drops its very last leaves. From the studio, I watched Osage leaves trickle by my high windows. All of the bittersweet leaves came down at the same time as the ginkgoes. Jeanie's redbud and another protected that had been protected by the white mulberry have dark, frost-burned foliage, but they still hang on.

2019: Deep cold penetrates into the soft days of yesterday's low-pressure system, the first significant snow of three inches and bitter wind. And so it seems to be the exact circumstance for the passage of the first sandhill cranes over Yellow Springs: Betty called at 2:33 excitedly announcing the first crane sighting of the season, fourteen right above High and Whiteman Streets.

2020: Clear, 32 degrees and frost on all the lawns, the warmth of the past week definitely gone. My white mulberry and Osage are the last holdouts in the neighborhood, towering, gilded in the morning sun. Numerous robins accompanied Jill and me on our walk to her house. At Ellis, the Sawtooth Oak holds its ochre leaves, the Swamp Chestnut Oak holds its chocolate-brown, wrinkled leaves. The sycamores are about bare. In the greenhouse, the first Christmas cactus, a red one, has started to bloom.

2022: First measurable snow, about two inches, fog and gray throughout the day. Four large murmurations of starlings seen about dawn as I drove to Cincinnati, another flock covering a cornfield on my return. Wet snow on all the evergreens and remaining honeysuckles brighten the roadsides. All the Christmas cacti in the greenhouse are opening.

2023: Robinsong, easy sing-song chanting at 7:00 this morning. The backyard Osage and the white mulberry still hold most of their leaves at pale green, some honeysuckle hedges in the woods yellow green, others around the house still dark summer green.

It is a mid-November litany
I did just yesterday in the warm, low sun
(pray for us),
to the zinnias surviving out of season,
late bumblebees and the newborn flies,
(pray for us),
Jeanie's roses still blooming,
cucumber beetles still mating in their folds
(pray for us),

grasshoppers still hopping,
crickets in the woods,
tree frogs sluggish in the wetlands,
(pray for us),
cabbage worms on the collards,
one cabbage butterfly still laying eggs
(pray for us),
yellow leaves holding to the Osage tree
and the white mulberry tree
(pray for us),
autumn violets open in the grass
(pray for us)

bf

November 13th
The 317th Day of the Year

Again the wind
Flakes gold-leaf from the trees
And the painting darkens –
As if a thousand penitents
Kissed an icon
Till it thinned
Back to bare wood
Without diminishment.

Jane Hirshfield, from "The October Palace"

Sunrise/set: 7:17/5:21
Day's Length: 10 hours 4 minutes
Average High/Low: 52/34
Average Temperature: 43
Record High: 75 – 1909
Record Low: 13 – 1911, 7 – 2019

The Daily Weather

Highs are in the 70s five percent of the afternoons, in the 60s twenty-five percent, in the 50s twenty-five percent, in the 40s twenty percent, 30s twenty percent, and, for the first time in the fall, in the 20s five percent of the time. The sun shines 75 percent of the days, frost strikes 65 percent of the mornings, rain falls 20 percent of the time, snow ten percent.

The Natural Calendar

New winter grain turns fields emerald green again in mild Novembers. Lawns grow back; they can be long and thick beneath the fallen leaves. Garlic mustard, sweet rocket, dock, hemlock and chickweed wait for April all across the woodland floor.

In the swamp during warmer years, fresh greens grow up from around the pale dead grasses. Protected by the stable temperature of streams, watercress brightens. Dock and ragwort come back around it, even when the air is bitter cold.

Driving south from Chicago, you can still find early fall,

113

catching up with the best of leafturn in Arkansas. Along the Gulf coast, the trees still hold their foliage, and colors haven't even reached their peak. By the time you go south far enough to recapture middle summer, the monarch butterflies will almost be getting ready to start back north from Michoacan, Mexico, and robins will be restless to leave the Caribbean.

By the time the frost reaches Mobile, Alabama, it will be just about time for it to recede. By the time second spring is halted by snow and cold in Indiana, it will be reaching its fulfillment in Georgia. By the time the last leaves fall in the southern Appalachians during mid December, the first leaves will be emerging in Florida. The last day of harvest in Ohio will be the first day of planting a thousand miles south where the last wildflower of one year will be blooming beside the first of the next.\

Daybook

1983: All the white mulberry leaves were gone this morning. A third of the Osage left. In front of the church, frost killed the marigolds, but not the petunias.

1984: White mulberry leaves fell overnight.

1986: Late Fall comes in hard with near record-breaking cold. Killing frost takes the lettuce, beets, broccoli, and all the bedding plants. Most leaves on the forsythia badly burned. Honeysuckle leaves limp.

1987: Storm hit in the early morning. Sudden demise of all the pear foliage. The river is higher from the all the rains, and the leaves tumble in the muddy current, tips coming to the surface, then diving like feeding fish. The wet woods are glowing, even with the fast, heavy clouds overhead. They smell of the earth and spring.

1988: Half the pear leaves remain, all red and gold in the middle of a November heat wave. Sun dominates, even cirrus gone this afternoon. On a long ride, a few asters seen, petunias, mums. Rivers high, and the grass still green, an early April color, and some pastures richer, darker. Cabbage worms found on the kale. A dandelion bloomed in the yard. A maple here and there has held its leaves.

1990: Cardinal sings at 7:15 a.m. Geese fly over at 8:00. Sweet gum trees yellow and red, hold at half.

1991: A cardinal sings at 7:15 a.m.

1992: A fierce storm brings in deep cold. A cardinal sings at 6:50, clear above the wind.

1993: Walking past the Webb's house on Dayton Street, I noticed that their two witch hazels were in full bloom.

1997: The witch hazel is in full bloom. Maples suddenly collapse after the white mulberry. Sycamores, too. Sweet gum holds. Ginkgo down overnight at school. Beeches fine gold.

1999: Driving along the freeway, I caught a glimpse of a patch of bright flowers, either dandelions, or hawkweed or lost coltsfoot. The November heat wave continues, summer haze all across the horizon. Witch hazel blooming on Dayton Street.

2000: Gingko, Osage, sweet gum, quince, and birch leaves mostly gone, beech and English oak half fallen, pears reddening, one red mulberry bare, one at half.

2002: Crows heard before eight o'clock this morning, first crows heard in a long time. In the greenhouse, the jade tree started to flower today (will bloom on into January). Christmas cacti all open now. Along Xenia Avenue in Yellow Springs, and on into Wilmington, 30 miles south, the pear trees are yellow, red and gold, full color and falling.

2005: The lettuce in the garden is lush and strong. The purple clematis by the east fence has four flowers.

2010: To the Covered Bridge, 65 degrees, the sky filling with cirrus and altostratus as a cold wave approaches from the southwest, the sun, which was warm all day, now suddenly thinned then blocked by the fontal system. Seven vultures circling high. I walked through the field of goldenrod, wingstem, bull thistles and ironweed, all the flowers tufted and gray, leaves curled around their stalks. All the foliage down except the yellow green leaves of the honeysuckles along the river. Not a single flower in bloom.

2011: The summer deep green of the Annabelle hydrangea is blanching and the leaves are withering. Zelcova leaves are almost all down. Tim was sweeping the pear leaves from in front of the Underdog Cafe this morning. A flock of starlings over Dayton and Stafford Streets when I went out to buy croissants. Wind through the day.

2012: A crisp and frosty morning. Peggy's pear tree is a burnished red and gold. The beech along Dayton Street is half down now. I saw a small contingent of robins moving through the trees along Stafford Street.

2014: No robins heard or seen this morning. Peggy's pear and the Dayton Street beech are at the same point they were in 2012. Jeanie's river birch has lost most of its leaves, the remaining ones pale gold. The Osage is still mostly green. At Ellis Pond, the cypresses are shedding their rusty foliage, are maybe half bald. On the way to Fairborn, I saw a very large murder of crows going north from one cutover field to another. A sizable flock of starlings was feeding a little further on. Deep cold has penetrated well into the South.

2015: Walk before dawn, clear and upper 30s, the ground covered with ginkgo leaves pulled down in yesterday's hard wind, several cardinal calls along south High Street at 7:12, then crows to the north, then the cry of a red-tailed hawk from the northeast.

2016: Second hard frost of the autumn, the last of the castor bean plants frozen.

2017: I saw Rick Downtown, and he said he had lots of

hummingbird moths at his bee balm this past summer – and that he had heard tree frogs a few nights back. Nancy at the monastery said she had seen oodles of reddish woollybear caterpillars.

2019: Deep cold continues, geese huddling in the taller grass near Ellis, the pond with a thin layer of ice. The oaks and cypresses hold their foliage still.

2021: First snow in the night, half an inch outlining the Lenten rose foliage, white stars. To Cincinnati under gray skies, the tree lines dull except for the rust of the oaks and the burnished gold of the ubiquitous pear foliage and the occasional beech.

Journal

More than one naturalist has noted the similarities in March and November. Even nature seems confused throughout late autumn, encouraging new growth - a kind of second spring - as if there would be no winter interruption of that cycle.

Protected in the swamp near my village, water cress brightens as though April were only a month or so away; dock and ragwort grow back beside the dead field grasses. Waterleaf is filling up the bottomlands again. Celandine is blooming, and a few dandelions, some chickweed, some violets, too. Seeds sprout in rotting logs. Skunk cabbage has already pushed to the surface, and it is ready to flower if December is warm.

Riding leisurely south, you can still find early October, catching up with the best of leafturn in Arkansas. Along the Gulf coast, the trees still hold their leaves, and colors haven't even reached their peak. And by the time the frost reaches New Orleans, it will be just about time for it to recede from the north. By the time the very last leaves fall in Chicago in December, the first leaves of the new year will be emerging in Florida.

March and November are, in fact, not so far apart as they appear. Paper calendars measure time in just one way, the linear way of human history. There is another kind of time (among so many other kinds of time, of course) one more metronomic and tidal, one in which the same matter, pushed and pulled by the moon, advances and retreats. In that rhythm, the seasons are stripped of their Gregorian sequence.

Those seasons do not compute the limited span of my life. They are not confined by space; they have no meaningful borders. They do not follow the sun. All of their successions feel reversible and illusory to me, metaphoric and prophetic. At best, their commencements are their closures – if I can feel them at all.

There is in all visible things an invisible fecundity, a dimmed light, a meek namelessness, a hidden wholeness.... There is in all things an inexhaustible sweetness and purity, a silence that is a fount of action and joy. It rises up in wordless gentleness and flows out to me from the unseen roots of all created being, welcoming me tenderly, saluting me with indescribable humility.

Thomas Merton

November 14th
The 318th Day of the Year

Each thing a certain course and lawes obeyes,
Striving to turne backe to his proper place;
Nor any settled order can be found,
But that which doth within itselfe embrace
The births and ends of all things in a round.

Boethius

Sunrise/set: 7:19/5:20
Day's Length: 10 hours 1 minute
Average High/Low: 51/34
Average Temperature: 43
Record High: 76 – 1909
Record Low: 17 – 1916

The Daily Weather

Chances of a high in the 60s are 40 percent today; temperatures reach the 50s on 20 percent of the afternoons, remain in the 40s fifteen percent of the time, and are in the 30s twenty-five percent. The sun appears six days in a decade; odds for frost are the same. Rain stays away three-fourths of the days, and flurries are rare.

The Natural Calendar

With most of the leaves down, the countdown for spring is underway. One might count in all sorts of ways. One method is to keep track of the number of precipitation days: about 50 days of rain or snow lie between now and April.

Another gauge is the number cloudy days: there are almost never more than 75, rarely fewer than 60. Or one could monitor the number of completely sunny days: there are usually about 30 (with a ten day margin for error) between the final goldenrod and the first hepatica.

Another way to judge the advance of winter is an enumeration of cold fronts: there will be around 30 in all, 20 of which will coincide with changes in the phase of the moon. If you

119

track these fronts on your barometer, graphing the ups and downs on a piece of paper, you will actually see them like waves finally bringing you to the warm shore of spring.

Even in the coldest spells of Deep Winter, the countdown can be made with a measurement of the depth of the sun's intrusion into your home through a south window. If you start today, you can watch the sun reach deeper and deeper inside until it slows and stops six weeks from now. The deeper it goes, the more dramatic its retreat after Christmas. If you mark its progress every few days with a pencil you will have a trail to follow next year, all the way to June.

Daybook

1982: Mums still blooming. More roadside grass is turning brown. Only a few leaves are left on the silver olives. Goldfinch seen, winter brown. Cardinals sang today.

1984: After this morning's frost, the stems of the salvia exploded with cold. South Glen: One dandelion in bloom. New leafcup foliage is a foot tall now beside lush sweet rocket and hemlock. Eastern burning bush discovered in the woods, its red berries showing in the wind. A flock of blackbirds in the sycamores across the road. Most all Osage leaves gone now, some rose foliage holding on, rose hips more prominent. Osage fruits yellowing. Zigzag leaves purple with frost, seeds puffed, white. In the greenhouse, one jade tree is blooming.

1985: Honeysuckle leaves in the yard drop suddenly. Lil's tree almost gone, like most of the ginkgoes. Gum tree still keeps a few red leaves. Osage and mulberry spot the tree line with yellow green. The cherry in the back yard is golden, full color, pecan turning gold, Jeanie's birch is half beige, downtown pears burnished. Some purple deadnettle budding in the garden.

1986: Cardinal sings at 7:00 a.m.

1987: 4:15 p.m., Sycamore Hole: River very low and clear. Three chubs caught, one two-pound carp. While I fished, I heard a bobwhite call from over near the Covered Bridge; a kingfisher raced back and forth along the shore a few times. All leaves are gone now including the pear leaves.

1990: Dogwoods with red berries, most of their pink leaves gone. Red berries on the flowering crabs, and on the hawthorns, on the honeysuckles, on the bayberry, hips on the roses: it's the season of red berries.

1992: My indoor cricket is quiet this morning. Outside, the day is silent too, except for a low growl from the northwest wind. After dawn, I heard crows and sparrows, but now they're gone. The first Christmas cactus flower began to open yesterday; it's completely unraveled today.

1993: Some of the late-blooming mums still hold on in the south garden, but they are bedraggled and should be cut back. Even the youngest Queen Anne's lace has turned black now. The astilbe foliage in the east garden has finally withered. Only two rose buds left along the north garden wall. Along the sidewalk, the forsythia is still solid, most of its leaves a violet gray.

1995: Except for the pears and the beeches, a few silver maples, the low forsythia and honeysuckle, most of the leaf-drop is complete. Frost is becoming common on the grass. Crows call in the morning, but otherwise the land seems still and bare.

1998: I am up at six sitting in the greenhouse. The sky is half dawn, light and dark equal through the fast gray nimbostratus clouds and the storm. The wind is hard from the southeast. The pattern of the gusts and rain creates a shape of its own, harsh like pebbles or hail, then soft, sweeping and blending, retreating.

After a few minutes, quiet. Then more squalls come pelting the house, surging at me passionately, pushing towards my chair, the sound measuring the speed, the size and quantity of the force. The most savage attacks shatter the raindrops against the window. My excitement increases with the intensity of the pounding that almost becomes too fervent, and I am growing restless kept at this high climactic plateau.

Then the pressure suddenly eases, the cloudburst ends. I

can see the tall cottonwoods swaying a block away, and instead of the wind given voice and revealed by the rain, instead of its insistent drumming and clattering, I hear it rushing in the bare branches and singing in the crevices and corners of the buildings and the fences around me. A few feet from where I sit, chickadees dive and hang at the feeders, glide with the rhythm of the air, at ease in the swells of the wind.

A small leak in the roof lets an intermittent drip of water fall on the indoor plants. The intrusion keeps a different time than that of the wind and rain outside, measuring how warm and dry and still I am here, surrounded by yellow pine and old brick, with a fire in the wood stove, and red and lavender geraniums and impatiens, all the silent warmth of summer collected and safe.

1999: Crows at 7:20 a.m. Half the beech leaves are gone. The white mulberry still holds in the morning, still partial to this record warm November; then in the afternoon, its leaves start coming down more quickly.

2000: Camel cricket found in the greenhouse. Around the yard, honeysuckles down to about a third. At school, magnolias three-fourths gone, Japanese maple half fallen. A few ginkgoes still have leaves. Some sweet gums are bare, but a few still keep most of their deep red leaves.

2005: Robins feeding on honeysuckle berries and whinnying in the High-Stafford Street alley, cardinal calling, when I walked with Bella there at 7:45. Osage and white mulberry leaves hold throughout the neighborhood. Beech rich golden brown keeps its leaves.

2006: I thought the beeches and pears were all falling a couple of days ago. Now I see they've held on, red-orange-gold throughout town and the countryside. A camel cricket was sitting on the wall by our bed tonight; I took it to the greenhouse.

2007: The Danielsons' and Mrs. Timberlake's maples are down, and Lil's keeps only a few leaves. The pears and peaches are full red and orange gold. In the past week, the honeysuckle and the river birch leaves have thinned dramatically, and all the Korean lilac leaves came down. Don's burning bush has started to shed, but at the strip mall plantings, the decorative red maples and the complementary rows of burning bush shrubs are still full bright red.

2009: Peter Hayes reported seeing juncos around this date.

2010: Robins peeping near dawn. Jimmy's maple and Dons suddenly shedding, Lil's keeping its shriveled leaves. In the overnight rain, at least half of the second phase of the white mulberry foliage came down, cluttering the smooth green of my mowed lawn. The cherry tree is just about bare, and the river birch is soft yellow and fragile. Downtown, the pear trees are burnished red, gold and green. From South Carolina, nephew John reports cool, foggy mornings, warm afternoons, catfish biting from about 8:00 a.m. to noon. This evening, I found four medium-size camel crickets when I was cleaning out the cat box in the greenhouse. From Springfield, Missouri, Jeffery Goss, Jr. writes: "Small flocks of craneflies beginning to appear."

2011: A man at the bank reported seeing a praying mantis today. Someone else said that they'd seen a walking stick "just the other day." I put in fifty tulips in the south garden this mild and windy afternoon.

2015: Frost on the car windshield, but there hasn't really been a hard freeze yet (just enough freezes to burn the annuals). A robin was peeping in the honeysuckles this morning. On the way to Cincinnati, I saw that many pear trees were rusty red. Across the street, the youngest Norway maple still keeps maybe a third of its leaves.

2016: A third morning of frost in a row, thanks to full moon and lunar perigee (a supermoon), but I saw a yellow sulphur crossing Ellis Pond around noon. Along Xenia Avenue, the ginkgoes are shedding, but still keep most of their leaves, the same as the white mulberry in the backyard. The downtown Zelcovas keep their lower foliage, rust brown. The Dayton-Street beech has just a few patches of orange.

2017: Allium and Dutch iris planted in the circle garden this afternoon, the back area pretty much ready for spring. The downtown pear trees are aging in green-yellow-browns, with none of the vibrancy of some years, Zelcovas still full and rusty brown, Lil's tree at about two-thirds down, the last holdout on High Street. Her burning bush is shedding quickly, too.

2019: Lil's maple burned and brown but holding at about a third to a half. Crows heard at 7:05 this morning and a vast murder of them seen west of Ellis Pond this afternoon. The number of geese seems to continue to grow across the road from the pond..

2020: Another morning of frost. I woke up to find the white mulberry in the backyard had lost about half its remaining leaves in the night. I waited for the collapse all day, but only a thinning took place in gentle warming. Large flock starlings seen over Dayton-Yellow Springs Road as we drove home from Koogler Fen in the late afternoon.

2021: The second snow of the year, steady throughout much of the day. The leaves of the pink quince have come down in and around the pond. The withered hackberry foliage fell yesterday, Jeanie's river birch and the red leaves of the north garden viburnum gone today. The snow collects on the front forsythia bushes and the tangles of Japanese honeysuckle, enhancing the barrier that remains to the street.

2022: Casey called: one bald eagle sighted near Ellis Pond.

....thereby I might se very wel, the whole nature of the wynde as it blewe that daye. And I had a great delyte and pleasure to mark it, which maketh me now far better to remember it.

Roger Ascham, 16th Century

November 15th
The 319th Day of the Year

If you are afflicted with melancholy at this season, go to the swamp and see the brave spears of skunk cabbage buds already advanced toward a new year.... See those green cabbage buds lifting the dry leaves in that watery and muddy place.... They see over the brown of winter's hill. They see another summer ahead.

Henry David Thoreau

Sunrise/set: 7:20/5:19
Day's Length: 9 hours 59 minutes
Average High/Low: 51/34
Average Temperature: 42
Record High: 74 – 1909
Record Low: 13 – 1916

The Daily Weather

Overcast conditions are the rule at the beginning of the third week of November, the sun failing to appear 60 percent of the time. Rain falls 60 percent of all the years too, and snow comes ten percent. Highs reach the 60s three days out of ten, the 50s two days in ten, the 40s two days, the 30s three days. Morning lows drop below freezing more than half the time.

The Weather in the Week Ahead

The 15th, 19th, and 20th are the days this week most likely to be mild with highs in the 60s. The fifth cold front of the month comes through at the end of the period, and the 21st brings a slight possibility for a high only in the 20s. The 15th is the day most likely to bring precipitation, having a 60 percent chance of rain or snow. The 20th is also fairly damp, carrying a 50 percent chance. The 18th is the driest day of the week; it has only a 20 percent chance of showers or flurries.

The Natural Calendar

Finches work the sweet gum trees, digging out the seeds from their hollows. Sparrow hawks appear on the fences, watching for mice in the bare fields. The last daddy longlegs huddle together woodpiles and brambles. In the warmest years, mosquitoes still wait for prey near backwaters and puddles. Late woolly bear caterpillars, most of them dark orange and black, still emerge in the sun. Cabbage butterflies and sulphurs look for the latest flowers.

Daybook

1983: Poplars turning, but their leaves hold on, along with the leaves of a few silver maples. Viburnum outside my building is still bright green.

1984: Mountain maples at Antioch more than half down. Magnolia leaves on the tree by my door: all but 20 dropped yesterday.

1987: Cardinal sang 11:25 a.m. A small carp, two chubs caught in the late afternoon at Sycamore Hole, Sun dropping quickly behind the trees.

1988: Mill Habitat, 55 degrees: Crickets and cardinals singing, a snake sunning on the path near the dam, flies, moths, and honeybees out. Hills of yellow-green honeysuckle, the color of second spring; above them turquoise sky, reflecting in the river. Saw my first squirrel eating Osage fruit, had always just seen the remnants, the results of their scavenging. A great blue heron flew upstream, chickadees, nuthatches chattering. Occasional dandelions blossoming. At home, mother-of-millions heads up to bloom.

1989: Geese fly over just before sunset.

1990: At Caesar Creek, temperatures near 70, pure sun and south wind for a trip upstream. Water low and clear, quiet, brown and blue. On the lake, hundreds of sea gulls, some loons and black ducks. In the greenhouse, the first Christmas cactus flowers. In the back yard, the white mulberry still keeps its leaves. Some ginkgoes still hold on in town, and the decorative pear leaves are red and beginning to fall. Cardinals have been calling a little each morning before dawn, but then they become quiet. Geese fly over every evening just before sunset. Most leaves are gone now except for the honeysuckle. A few crickets are still singing.

1991: Sparrows swarm in the schoolyard, pigeons circle the tower at Wilberforce.

1992: Cold, quiet morning, half an inch of snow on the ground, nothing moves outside. This afternoon: honeysuckle leaves fall quickly now, lilac thinned to just an upper core.

1993: Decorative pears along Xenia Avenue and Dayton Street are a full deep gold. The leaves are gone from the red jewel crabapples.

1997: The Osage leaves have almost all come down now, the honeysuckle very thin, most of the mock orange fallen. Lilacs hold at maybe half. First real snow today, but only a little sticks.

1999: The white mulberry in the back yard sheds more. At Wilberforce, my ginkgo is still yellow green, hardly beginning leafdrop, the latest it has ever held its leaves (and the ash held far longer than usual this year too). The other ginkgo is shedding, but still has maybe half its foliage.

2000: My library Japanese maple in Springfield sheds all but a third of its leaves. Still fragments of burning bush beside it.

2003: To northern Ohio in light rain with a light southwest wind: The roadside grass was losing its color. The trees – all but a few willows and silver maples – were bare. Only the honeysuckles and evergreens gave life to the fencerows and yards. Winter wheat was deep emerald green, but it had none of the luster that characterized it on sunny days earlier in the fall. The ponds were dull and gray, the newly plowed fields dark and sodden. I saw only two crows, a small flock of sparrows, and one medium- sized flock of starlings during the entire 320-mile trip.

2006: The front honeysuckle is bare: only red berries there, a sign of the early approach of Early Winter. Hosta breakdown continues, leaves disappearing quickly into the ground. Stonecrop diminishing, shrinking, falling. Lilac leaves maybe half down. Jerry and Lee's sweet gum two-thirds down, golden.

2007: The young maple in the boulevard by the driveway has finally come down; it parallels Lil's tree, is maybe one of its children. The viburnum by the north side of the house has lost most of its trees. The hostas continue to yellow, following last year's schedule. I put a cover over the pond, anticipating the quince leafdrop – its leaves all yellow-gold, but the northwest wind has kept them to the south of the pond. At Wilberforce, my ginkgoes are pale yellow green, but hold most of their leaves.

2008: Frank's silver maples are shedding rapidly now, and Late Fall deepens with rust overtaking most of the beech tree on Dayton Street; red and gold are spreading through the pears. In the mornings, robins peeping all around the yard. Quince leaves are completely down, the pond pretty clear of debris. Hostas are dissolving into the soil. The first snowfall came today, huge fat flakes covering the forsythia and the ground for an hour or so.

2009: Another day in the 60s, soft, overcast sky. The white mulberry continues to trickle down after losing half its leaves in a few hours several days ago. The winterberries are white and orange, the color at their peak. Beside the secret maple, a burning bush holds its pale, red leaves.

2010: Venus was just visible over the tree line at 5:45 a.m. beginning its long reign as morning star of the new natural year. Crisp and frosty this morning early, but rapid transformation into high cirrus and altostratus by midmorning. The Dayton Street beech is half down, all the silver maples and the sweet gums pretty well fallen. The Osage leaves have not started to come down yet, but by the river all their foliage is gone. Along the highway to Springfield, one Osage tree with fruits all around it, the balls already turning yellow. The hostas by the back shed are spreading their pods, showing all their black seeds. Along High Street, the bittersweet leaves and seed hulls are dropping now. As I walked Bella at 10:00 this morning, a cardinal was singing and singing, and clusters of starlings whistled far away. The news talked of a foot of snow in Minneapolis.

This afternoon, Jane Britton wrote from Columbia, South Carolina:

"Here in Columbia, SC, we've had no frost yet, and the leaves on the crepe myrtles, dogwoods, and most of the native trees are at their brilliant peak. Last week was the most beautiful 'Indian Summer' in recent memory, with cool nights in the 30s and daily highs in the 70s, and brilliant clear blue skies. In our yard, the last of my pink "old roses" are blooming, along with a pink *Camellia sasanqua*, and a patch of wild *Ageratum* and *Physostegia*. The stark contrast between the bright autumn leaves and the last explosion of pinks and purples throws my garden design into disarray, but they are all beautiful. My office at work looks out onto the grounds of the State Capitol building, whose grounds are a beautiful park, containing many old specimens of native, as well has other, plants. I always enjoy observing the gingko trees, which have only slight twinges of gold now. We are fortunate to have the Congaree National Park in our backyard, and spent yesterday morning 'in the swamp.' The cypress trees are copper, and haven't begun to shed. The tupelo gums are just beginning to change. We saw whole posses of green anoles warming themselves on the trunks of fallen trees, and feasting on the insects there. The crickets provided the soundtrack, along with the many birds that are there. The birds make occasional forays into our backyard where they have planted an entire border of native plants and shrubs."

2011: All the ginkgoes are down after two windy and rainy days. The oakleaf hydrangeas are becoming fully red and purple, and the goosefoot foliage in the garden is a blend of gold and yellow and red and violet. A great flock of blackbirds was heading north as we drove back from Beavercreek this afternoon. One female finch came to the feeder today, the first finch since we put the new seed up.

2014: Last night, temperature in the teens, brought the Osage foliage (except for the leaves on one branch) all at once.

2015: Jeanie's redbud, the last in the yard, finally dropped its leaves today.

2016: The bittersweet vine has kept many of its leaves, winds around the bare redbud, pale orange berries prominent now, a few honeysuckle berries red beside them. The ginkgo near Jill's house shed its leaves yesterday. My Osage and my white mulberry tree keeping their foliage. At 12:26 this afternoon, full sun, mild in the upper 50s: a lone monarch crossed the north garden heading southwest (the latest I've seen one here to date).

2017: Lil's maple about three-fourths down, the Dayton Street beech deep brown and about a third down. I cut back the last melted hosta leaves in the east garden.

2018: Wildfires burn California. A storm here, trees and shrubs bowed with ice and snow, sweet gums and honeysuckles especially affected since they still have many of their leaves. All the bamboo has collapsed into the pond. The oaks sag, but hold up the best. The remaining redbud and maple foliage is twisted and frozen. A definitive punctuation to the last phase of Late Fall. A small flock of starlings settles in the Stafford Street trees in the morning. From Corning in New York, Lois sends photos of her porch railing with eight inches of snow.

2020: Hurricane Iota heads to Central America. Hard winds in the middle of clouds and sun this afternoon, strip almost all the last white mulberry leaves from my tree, and they thin the last Osage at the southwest edge of the yard. All the leaves from Lil's tree have been blown across the street, filling my front sidewalk.

2023: Robins still chirping and chitterig at first light. Blue jays still present, but no longer loud and aggressive. Jill reports another large flock of starlings near the freeway this afternoon, her third sighting in the past ten days. The is yard becomes browner now as the undergrowth settles back for winter. Honeysuckles and white mulberry leaves turn to a canvas-like ochre, are ready to collapse. I cut back the sedum yesterday, seed heads black from age and frost. Mice invading the house: nine captured in the live trap this week. Jill still reports Asian lady beetles in her vestibule. And Jeff called this afteroon after returnig home from being with his sister Linda, who died just after he left. Thin time. (Does the Daybook simply end when I and the other characters die? Of course. Which entry will be the last?)

Journal

In spite of a spiritual imperative, articulated in the call of the geese and the robins, to abandon the cold, I am spending winter in the north again. I have done my raking for the year. The strawberries are covered with straw. The pumpkins are aging, and the apple cider is made. The garden is filled with manure. Sweet Williams, spinach and onions are planted and covered for April.

With summer scattered and withered, I count each of my allies, from my wife and daughters to the birds at the sunflowers. The tropical plants I have inside the greenhouse are budding, needing care and reminding me of choices I have made. It is too late to run, to merge into the flyway corridor away from January. I am committed to solstice and to the next quarter into equinox.

After the nostalgia that accompanies the migrations and the sadness of leaf fall, my brain receives new signals, defiance and a call to survive. I am already counting days, attempting to demystify the time ahead. Thirty-five days to solstice, 65 to the center of winter, 100 to the first hours of early spring. A finite, divided winter is already mastered. Soon it will seem too short, I tell myself, the hibernation not long enough.

Garlic mustard is already waiting all across the woodland floor. It sprouted fourteen months ago and has persevered with only a cluster of basal leaves all summer. The worst freeze will not kill it. It is ready for the end of April. There is a faith in its roots, a knowledge I can use against my suspicion that the end of the year mirrors too closely the end of human existence. Far wiser things than I have absolute faith. They give promises the Sun has and will come back again.

Storms and the snows arrive to test the woodpile and my fantasy of self-sufficiency. The corner is turned. The grieving for summer and fall are over quickly. In a few weeks, it is no surprise to see bare branches. I look for what is there instead of what is gone.

Christmas cactus blossoms and aloe spikes rise to bloom in the early December greenhouse. Paperwhites send up their foliage. My violet hibiscus blossoms, remembering some tropical dictate, faithful here, finding just the right amount of light to make its seeds. In the sun, the starlings, staying here within reach of my safe feeder, swing in the back trees. Window parsley is growing new leaves. I go out collecting second-spring foliage from sweet Cicely, chickweed, sweet rockets, waterleaf, cinquefoil, violet cress, hemlock, parsnip, avens and next September's zigzag goldenrod.

There are days when it could be March, hazy skies, cardinals singing, temperatures in the warm 50s. I walk the swamp and find Thoreau's "brave spears of the skunk cabbage, buds already advanced toward a new year.

"They see over the brown of winter's hill," Henry David promises my doubts. "They see another summer ahead."

In the autumn days, the creaking of crickets is heard at noon over all the land, and as in summer they are heard chiefly at nightfall, so then by their incessant chirp they usher in the evening of the year. Nor can all the anxieties that vex the world alter one whit the measure that night has chosen. Every pulse beat is in exact time with the cricket's chant and the tickings of the death watch in the wall. Alternate with these if you can.

Henry David Thoreau

November 16th
The 320th Day of the Year

November sun is sunlight poured through honey:
Old things, in such light, grow subtle and fine,
Bare oaks are like still fire.

Conrad Aiken

Sunrise/set: 7:21/5:18
Day's Length: 9 hours 57 minutes
Average High/Low: 50/34
Average Temperature: 42
Record High: 73 – 1930
Record Low: 8 – 1883

The Daily Weather

Chances of precipitation drop from yesterday's 60 percent down to 30 percent, and the sun shines half of the days in my record. Temperatures reach the 70s five percent of the years, are in the 60s ten percent, 50s forty percent, 40s twenty percent, 30s twenty-five percent. Snow falls once in a decade. Lows in the single digits become a possibility, but lows still remain above freezing a little more than half the time.

The Natural Calendar

Now the inventory of the neighborhood year rests on a count of the remaining leaves on trees or plants, the breakdown of the fallen leaves, the subtlety of the last colors, the coming apart of seed heads, the disappearance of berries.

The silver maples and the oaks thin out. Forsythia turns deep red and gold from frost. Poplars shrivel. Most mock orange leaves and most of the lilacs are gone. Sometimes half the ginkgo seeds hang on above the golden skirt of their fallen foliage; often they have all come down.

Late Fall deepens with rust overtaking most of the beech tree on Dayton Street; red and gold are spreading through the pears. Osage fruits are almost all on the ground, stand out chartreuse, at random, in the tangle of the undergrowth. Cypress trees have thinned, their branches a delicate web against the sky. Pink coralberries glow in the hedges. Bittersweet berries crack and reveal their softer cores. The foliage of black-eyed Susans is gray, flower petals gone, centers so black. Silver olive leaves have fallen.

There are red berries on the flowering crabs, on the dogwoods, and on the hawthorns, on the honeysuckles, on the bayberry, red hips on the roses, bittersweet hulls on the sidewalk, white exteriors of euonymus berries splitting, revealing the orange cores. Stems of salvia have exploded from the cold. Hostas dissolve into the soil.

Garden lettuce, rhubarb and comfrey are prostrate in the cold. Hydrangea and mock orange leaves are curled and blackened. Finches work the sweet gum trees, digging out the seeds from their hollows. The last daddy longlegs huddle together woodpiles and brambles. Late woolly bear caterpillars, most of them dark orange and black, still emerge in the sun. Juncos arrive for winter. In the mornings, robins peeping all around the village. Geese continue to gather at the pond.

The oakleaf hydrangeas are becoming dusky purple, and the goosefoot foliage in the garden is a blend of gold and yellow and red and violet. New leafcup foliage is a foot tall now beside lush sweet rocket and hemlock. Some purple deadnettle is budding.

Christmas cactus blossoms and aloe spikes rise to bloom in the early December greenhouse. Paperwhites send up their foliage.. Foliage from sweet Cicely, chickweed, sweet rockets, waterleaf, cinquefoil, violet cress, hemlock, parsnip, avens and next September's zigzag goldenrod in a defiant show of Second Spring.

Daybook

1983: Oaks seem older, darker, thinner. Forsythia turning gold, red, yellow. Osage losing more leaves. Poplars in the yard burned and shriveled from the cold. Mock orange keeps most of its leaves.

1984: Seven magnolia leaves left at the west wall of my building in Wilberforce. Some silver maples have almost all their leaves.

1985: Our cherry tree lost all its leaves overnight.

1986: Fishing at Sycamore Hole: bobwhites, starlings, flocks of geese. Full moon day: two chubs, two shiners caught, some carp biting.

1987: Sycamore Hole: two chubs at 5:15 this afternoon, warm 60-degrees, some carp biting too.

1988: Violets still blooming along Corry Street. Cardinals sing in the 60-degree morning, wind and rain.

1992: Mums damaged now by snow and lows in the lower 20s. Honeysuckle leaves three-fourths fallen. Most oaks gone. Most mock orange gone, a few last lilac leaves hang on.

1994: No hard freeze yet. Information I have from the Xenia weather station suggests that a killing frost has occurred by the third week of November better than 98 percent of the time. November 25th is the latest date for such frost in central Ohio, and if we can get past the cold fronts of the 18th and the 24th, we'll exceed that date maybe by as much as five to ten days.

1997: No birds at all this morning, not even crows. A dusting of snow on the ground today; I raked the yard a little bit anyway, the leaves wet but crisp from the cold. Collars set around the roses. In the garden, kale, cabbage and chard have survived the gray and cold. A few new weeds have sprouted here and there. This afternoon, a fly was trying to get out of the greenhouse.

1998: Poplars and lilacs hold at about a third. Crows quieter the past two weeks.

1999: Today I read back over the mid-March daybook, and I look outside to the same landscape, and I imagine spring and myself there.

2000: In the late autumn rain, I watch the apple tree that stands outside my back door. The tree has become a gnomon for me, a measure of the seasons and years. It has grown here for almost a century, and now it's dying.

The rain is slow and soft. At the base of the tree, the fallen apples have decayed. The yellow jackets and the bumblebees that loved them are gone. Hostas in the apple garden are tawny, seedpods brittle and empty.

To my right, the locust and the box elder are bare, and the white mulberry is yellowing. On my left, the Osage is gold, fruits down on the woodpile. Honeysuckles are weakening all around the yard, showing their red berries. In front of them, the asters from September are gone, along with the ironweed, the butterfly bushes, summer lilies, blue iris, tulips, daffodils.

Cars hiss by on Dayton Street. A squirrel is chattering. Crows come to the woodlot west of my back door. I think about the long flock of blackbirds that flew over yesterday morning. Last night, I heard just one whistling cricket.

The full moon always sets through the arms of the apple tree, sometimes a little to the left, sometimes a little to the right. At winter solstice, the sun disappears below the horizon in its southern branches, at summer solstice in its northern branches, at March and September equinox dead center on the rotting trunk.

2002: In Dayton, the ginkgoes near the University of Dayton hold at half, even though the Yellow Springs ginkgoes fell on schedule.

2003: A loud cardinal interrupted my reading at 7:02 this morning. When I went out near 9:00, I could hear robins and grackles in the distance.

2005: First snowflakes of the year as a hard cold front cuts across the Midwest (tornadoes all across the Border States – the third or fourth such event this month). To Switzerland County, 100 miles southwest of Yellow Springs: The hills were brown, freeway grass still quite green, honeysuckles thinning, yellow green below the bare canopy. A few white mulberry and Osage, still intact, scattered here and there. Pear leaves still green and holding most places. One bedraggled ginkgo kept most of its leaves in Vevay. Bennington Road was green and glowing in the low, gray sky, the pastures rich and the roadsides promising April.

2007: More and more flocks of starlings seen as I drive to Dayton, large flocks, small flocks. Elephant ears finally burned by more intense frost last night.

2009: The beech on Dayton Street is empty, and Peggy's pear tree is shedding. Driving south to the paper store, we saw all the honeysuckles yellow and thinning. The crop report I received today said that the second week of November this year had been seven and a half degrees above normal. Although there have been two or three light freezes, killing annuals and withering some leaves, there has been no serious frost yet. As I walked Bella tonight, soft distant field cricket song.

2010: An all-afternoon rain soaks the Ohio Valley for the first time in weeks. John, arriving from fishing at Santee-Cooper, told about the inconsistent catfish biting patterns, but also about catching his first 22-pounder last night.

2011: Rain for two days, mild in the 50s. The beech on Dayton Street is almost bare. Pear trees along Xenia Avenue are half down, colder and windier weather becoming the norm now. The white mulberry tree and the Osage tree are shedding slowly this year, no violent collapse as has happened many times in the past.

2012: A large flock of starlings has settled over the west end of the village this midmorning. Occasional robin chirps, sparrow chatter around me as I stand looking up into the trees. Along Dayton Street, the beech has lost all but its lower leaves. Downtown, the pear trees are full burnished gold and shedding. The post office Zelcova has been down for a while, but others along Xenia Avenue still hold copper-brown. At Ellis Pond, the sawtooth oak is yellowing more and more, and the weeping willow leaves have wrinkled and grayed from the daily heavy frosts. In the back yard, the oak leaf hydrangea leaves are deep red-brown-violet. The last mum, the red one with the yellow centers, has finally ceded to the cold. I cut down the last of the peony stems, raked the plot clean so I could see the red spears of the new year come up in February.

2014: Gray and cold in the 20s, light wind. One robin whinny as I walked Bella after breakfast. A handful of starlings sat in Carl's black walnut tree whistling and chattering. In the alley, some solitary starlings, some in groups of three. As in many years past, the white and green snow-on-the-mountain has grown back to about three inches high.

2015: Robins still peeping in the morning. No starlings in town, however. Even though the days have been warm, the pond water has chilled from the cold nights, and the koi were slow to feed this morning. From Umbria in central Italy, Neysa says that the persimmons have come in early this year, a lush crop, their persimmon tree laden with large fruit.

2016: After a week of chilly nights and sunny days, the koi are sluggish, don't seem interested in eating.

2018: Bittersweet hulls on the sidewalk near Limestone Street. They came down when the ice melted from the vines. Yellow Springs Creek: water bugs still spinning.

2020: Even after yesterday's winds, the mulberry keeps maybe a fourth of its leaves, orange in the morning sun, and the Osage seems unfazed by the storm. Several robins in the alley at dawn. This evening, Category 5 Hurricane Iota moves on Nicaragua.

2021: At Ellis this afternoon, over 200 Canadian geese counted on the pond. I had been worried they wouldn't come this year. But no starlings seen in the neighborhood trees, and no long flocks of blackbirds flying over.

2022: First overwintering red canna lily blooms beside the Christmas cacti. From Amsterdam in Holland, Trudy sends photos of her magnificent Christmas cactus collection.

2023: Rick writes: " Stepped out the back door this evening to see a small handful of cranes quietly fly over at around 1,000 ft. First I've seen for several years."

When after climbing the little winding lane up the hillside, I came out onto the open at the top, I could hardly realize how good it was to be out in the woods again, after months of denial. A dead weed, virgin's bower seeds with a little puff of snow on each cluster, how beautiful. I looked up into the vast gray sky, which was luminous with invisible sunlight behind the clouds, and felt: I am home again—this is mine.

Charles Burchfield, *Journal*

The stars are down close to the trees,
The air crisp, no wind, no cricket or bird.

August Derleth

Sunrise/set: 7:22/5:18
Day's Length: 9 hours 56 minutes
Average High/Low: 50/33
Average Temperature: 41
Record High: 78 – 1958
Record Low: 9 – 1959

The Daily Weather

Fifteen percent of the afternoons reach 60 degrees on this date in November, and 45 percent climb into the 50s. On the colder side, 40s occur 25 percent of the time, and 30s come 15 percent of the days. Rain falls 30 percent of the time, snow once in a decade. Lows reach below freezing about half of all the early mornings.

The Natural Calendar

The tracking of leafturn and leaf fall from specific trees offers a semblance of control to the tracker. And an annual record of the gradual transformation and shedding of those trees, often reveals the character of an entire year.

Like counting fallen leaves, however, the practice of recording the progress of autumn with arboreal landmarks may be simply an exercise in fantasy, a comforting pretense of lay scientific observation, as though the state of the Dayton Street beech or Lil's maple really mattered.

A game of fantasy or not, there does come a point at which the tracking seems to produce closure and to make sense: The branches are finally empty. The vigil was not in vain. The proof lets in the entire sky. The waiting is complete, and then the awareness of the passage of foliage becomes a different vigil, one that might seem more reasonable to some people, the vigil for spring.

As the buds swell and birds start to sing and wildflowers grow back, the tracker collects different kinds of pieces. When there are enough pieces, spring becomes the sum of its parts, heaping up the landscape to the top of May.

By the middle of November's third week, the sun passes a declination of 18 degrees and is now three-fourths of the way to winter solstice. Several hours after dark, summer's Hercules and Aquila are setting. Cassiopeia is moving east around Polaris, and the great dog star, Sirius, is visible at the tree line, its magnitude of -1.4 making it the brightest star in the night sky. The pointers of the Big Dipper point northeast-southwest. Andromeda is directly overhead; Pisces lies just below it to the south.

Daybook

1984: The last leaves fell from my star magnolias at the west wall today.

1985: South Glen: Flock of bluebirds at the butterfly preserve. According to my records, November 15th is the last departure date for bluebirds from Grand Lake, 100 miles north of here. Are these the last of the bluebirds? At home, Early Winter forsythia blossoms.

1988: A robin passes south through the yard. Forsythia thinning quickly to maybe a fourth of its summer foliage.

1989: White mulberry leaves fell all at once today after an inch and a half of rain, then cold north winds, snow. Forsythia hurt in a 15-degree morning low. Osage leaves hold.

1990: The last white mulberry leaves came down last night in the rain. Forsythia foliage holds at maybe three-fourths. Roses mulched today.

1991: Toward Dayton, starlings continue flocking and feeding in the fields, huge numbers flying back and forth. Sparrows loud in the pear trees (leaves holding at about two thirds). Most of the ginkgo seeds hang on. Greens fading from lawns and pastures;

there has been little rain this November, increasing cold.

1992: Beech almost gone on Dayton Street. I'm getting anxious for everything to be over, want the peace of winter, less change.

1993: The late maples on High Street came down this week. Bradford pears on Xenia Avenue are golden red, have just passed their prime and are beginning to fall, branches full of screeching sparrows. Dayton Street and Xenia Avenue are lined with bright red crab apples and hawthorn berries.

1994: Weeding in the strawberry beds, I found the purple deadnettle grown back to middle March levels, its foliage lush, but no buds yet.

1997: The pond froze over last night for the first time. The river was frozen at the edges, too.

1998: Silver olives along the highway 80 or 90 percent gone, honeysuckles half gone and yellowing. Tree line bare except for chocolate leaves of the oaks, and scattered maples.

1999: The last of the white mulberry leaves and the last of the red mulberry leaves came down today. The beech across the street: maybe a fourth left.

2000: Japanese maple at about a tenth of its foliage left, English oak at a third, beech at a fifth.

2001: A cardinal was singing when I walked out the back door at 7:03 this morning. Crows in the distance. Beeches more than half down on Dayton Street. Tonight one last whistling cricket in the hedge.

2002: The white mulberry leaves came down overnight. Across the landscape, only a few trees remain bright gold or red-orange. It is finally the middle of Late Fall.

2004: The beech on Dayton Street is full gold today. The white mulberry leaves in the back yard hang on at maybe ten or twenty percent; the sudden collapse of previous years did not occur this November.

2005: Deep freeze to 23 degrees, and the remaining white mulberry leaves were all over the back yard this morning. The Osage leaves were holding as of 8:00 a.m. In the afternoon, they were coming down. I dug some elephant ear bulbs, the ground not frozen yet.

2007: At the Glen art show, Chet, a man from Huber Heights, said that he had a rose-breasted nuthatch at his feeder last week, the only one he has ever had. Another person talked about seeing a giant flock of crows along Dayton-Yellow Springs Road this morning. Mateo's red mulberry is more than half fallen; mine along the south border has thinned, too. Janet's redbud lost its foliage at least a week ago; the others in the yard, the younger, more sheltered trees, still keep most of theirs.

2009: A cool morning, altostratus clouds except a low blue opening across the north. In the alley, the thin-leafed coneflower is still in full bloom, completing its cycle deliberately as though it were September.

2010: Around noon today, a huge flock of starlings stretched from High Street east along Dayton Street for several blocks. Down town, the pears are deep gold now and starting to shed. In the overnight rain, most of Jimmy's and Burl's maple leaves came down, and the second-last level of the white mulberry in the yard.
2011: Crows at 7:20 this morning, a large hawk seen on the phone wires along the highway south. And Jeanie said she saw another hawk sitting in the back trees today. Pear leaves shedding quickly on Xenia Avenue, white mulberry leaves coming down all day in the back yard.

2012: Crows at about 7:20. When I went out with Bella this morning about 10:15, a large flock of starlings was moving about in the High and Stafford Street trees. In the background a cardinal was singing. On the Limestone Street eaves, sparrows were chattering and bantering.

2013: Hard winds and rain this evening, tornadoes and straight-line wind destruction in Illinois and Indiana. After the storm, the sky was clear, the air crisp and firm in the breeze, the full moon so bright, Jupiter shining over Jerry and Lee's house in the northeast. One of the koi lies listless near the surface on the west end of the pond, seems like he is dying.

2014: At least six inches of snow throughout the village overnight, and deep lows expected tomorrow, should break the record. Tornadoes in the South as this severe cold front wars with Gulf warmth and moisture. This afternoon, Ed Oxley called, said he had seen thousands of crows assembled in the fields north and west of town. Low of 13 tonight, four degrees from the record.

2015: Robins peeping in the honeysuckles. The koi rise sluggishly to take their food. Solitary crickets still trill in the mild evenings as the barometer falls before a storm.

2016: A lone tree cricket remains unmoving on the glass of the studio door as I enter and leave.

2017: Walk before sunset along the bike path, the sky just clear enough to provide a dusky glow to the still green honeysuckle leaves and the burnished path sides and the second-spring watercress in the ditches. Winterberry quite prominent, red berries protruding from white shells, bittersweet vines all dried but berries holding all uncovered, one bush with coralberries. A large cluster of craneflies followed us for a while across the old soybean field. At Ellis, the red oaks deep brown.

2021: Lil's tree darkened and thinning quickly now, leaves curled. A basket-worth of large Osage fruits fell along High Street overnight. The bittersweet vine has climbed through the pussy willows and the redbuds, dangles its orange fruit above the sidewalk.

2022: Bittersweet shells falling to the sidewalk, replacing the honeysuckle berries in sequence. Orange winterberries protrude boldly through their hulls. I planted the last long-stemmed tulips in the backyard this afternoon, in flurries and temperature abouit 35 degrees.

Outside, everything has opened up. Winter clear-cuts and reseeds the easy way. Everywhere paths unclog... The woods are acres of sticks; I could walk to the Gulf of Mexico in a straight line. When the leaves fall, the striptease is over. Things stand mute and revealed. Everywhere skies extend, vistas deepen, walls become windows, doors open.

Annie Dillard

A man must attend to Nature closely for many years to know when, as well as where, to look for his objects, since he must always anticipate her a little. Young men have not learned the phases of Nature; they do not know what constitutes a year, or that one year is like another. I would know when in the year to expect certain thoughts and moods, as the sportsman knows how to look for plover.

Henry David Thoreau

Sunrise/set: 7:23/5:17
Length of Day: 9 hours 54 minutes
Average High/Low: 49/33
Average Temperature: 41
Record High: 75 – 1930 and 2016
Record Low: 10 – 2014

The Daily Weather

Highs reach 70 five percent of the time, climb into the 60s ten percent, into the 50s twenty percent, the 40s forty-five percent, the 30s fifteen percent, stay in the 20s or teens five percent. Chances are good there will be no precipitation: the 18th is one of the driest of November days: rain just once or twice in a decade, with the same possibilities for snow. The sun shines two days in three, and frost strikes a little more than half of the mornings.

The Natural Calendar

The silver maples and the oaks thin out. Forsythia turns deep red and gold from frost. Poplars shrivel. Most mock orange leaves and most of the lilacs are gone. Sometimes half the ginkgo seeds hang on above the golden skirt of their fallen foliage. The beeches and pears and willows weaken. Osage fruits are almost all down, stand out chartreuse, at random, in the tangle of the undergrowth. Cypress trees have thinned, their branches a delicate web against the sky. Pink coralberries glow in the hedges. Bittersweet berries crack and reveal their softer cores.

1983: Grinnell Swamp: one white aster blooming by the roadside. A few Osage leaves left. Honeysuckle yellowing, red berries still prominent. Cress, grasses, algae strong in the swamp, climbing bittersweet open, ferns bright, nestled with lichens, some new waterleaf, thimble plant puffed up and losing its seeds, a "walking fern" noticed deep green on the upper path rocks.

1985: Geese fly over at 8:00 a.m. and 5:00 p.m.

1986: First juncos seen.

1989: All leaves from the south poplar gone. Two blossoms open on the white Christmas cactus.

1990: Walk down Polecat Road at dawn, violet sky streaked with pink and red contrails and cirrus. Frost across the fields, black cattle in the gray-blue pasture. Geese and ducks going over. Then, from the west side of the railroad tracks, two shots from a shotgun, and a goose, flying to the left of one formation, veered down into the trees, crying out when it struck the branches.

1991: Geese still fly over the village. Starlings are still gathering at the back trees. A late flock of bluebirds passed by on the 17th.

1992: Some pear trees in the village are brown and losing leaves, but others are full green, untouched by Late Fall.

1993: At South Glen, the paths stay green in spite of the cold, contrasting with pale brown fields beside them. Osage fruits are almost all down, stand out chartreuse, surreal, at random along the river walk. One coralberry bush glows pink. In the lower prairie, a patch of black-eyed Susans with gray foliage, petals gone, centers so black. Silver olive leaves have fallen in the past week here. Downtown, the pear leaves come down quickly in the sun.

1994: Jacoby Swamp: October and November have been mild and sunny this year, and the forest floor looks like it does in spring.

Garlic mustard has grown four or five inches tall, its leaves wide and bright. Chickweed has come back all along the paths, cress in the pools and streams. Grasses are returning. Skunk cabbage is showing all over the swamp, some plants even opening a little. Today's sun sets the new plants glowing like they glow in April, and the blue sky and the intense green, the fresh scent in the air, one yellow sulphur butterfly at the landing, all say that it's spring.

1997: Sparrow hawk seen on the phone line along Wilberforce-Clifton Road this afternoon. Neysa reports the sparrows still chatter every morning in the pears outside her downtown apartment windows.

1998: To Springfield with Walt on the new bike path north: First juncos seen, red-bellied woodpecker, flocks of robins. Wild cherries fallen to the path. Golden bittersweet berries showing high in a leafless tree; their vine had escaped the path builders. The blue sky full of sweeping cirrus, mild southwest wind strong in our faces, as we came back to Yellow Springs.

2003: When I walked Bella down High Street this morning, I found that bittersweet had fallen to the sidewalk. When I looked at the vine tangled above me in the maple tree, all the red berries were showing inside their wide-open hulls. In Washington Court House, quite a few dandelions were blooming. This afternoon as I went out to the woodshed, an Asian ladybug flew in front of me heading for the honeysuckles.

2005: Hard frost yesterday and this morning. Bittersweet hulls on the sidewalk, white exteriors of euonymus berries splitting, revealing the orange cores. Lettuce, rhubarb and comfrey prostrate in the cold. Hydrangea and mock orange leaves curled and blackened. Ice on half the pond. Beech tree on Dayton Street and Jerry and Lees sweet gum are both about three-fourths gone. Dahlia bulbs dug today.

2006: In the park where I walk, the paths have stayed green in spite of the cold, contrasting with dull fields beside them. Osage fruits are almost all down, stand out chartreuse, surreal, at random along my river walk. I brush against a patch of black-eyed Susans with brittle foliage, petals gone, centers so black.

Yesterday, I saw the first juncos of the winter, their white breasts ready for snow. Golden bittersweet berries were showing, pushing out from their pale hulls, high in a leafless tree. Hydrangea and mock orange leaves were curled and blackened from frost. On my black walnut tree, only three of the walnuts remained, hanging alone, waiting for a storm. The blue sky was full of sweeping cirrus, southwest wind strong in my face.

Cleaning one of our closets, Jeanie found a family of camel crickets, two large and four small ones, living in an empty shoebox. When she picked up the box, the largest one jumped onto her sweater as though it were defending the family. Camel crickets, of course, bring good luck in winter, and she tucked them all safely in the greenhouse.

2007: Walking through the alley with Bella this morning about 9:15, I came across a small flock of starlings in the honeysuckle bushes, and several of the tall trees held larger groups of birds than usual. All but three of the Limestone Street black walnuts have fallen. All the leaves have come down from the trumpet vine, following the season of honeysuckle leafdrop.

Thirty years ago, most turkey vultures left the Glen by the first week of November. Some years since then, especially in the 21st century, the vultures have been seen throughout the winter. Local naturalist Ruby Nicholson sent me this observation on the buzzards of 2007: "At 4:15 p.m., November 18, I was on President Street near Cory Street. Nearby was a tree covered with buzzards. I began counting on the east side of the tree and ending on the west: 68 and the critters were still coming in when I left. One hour later, only three remained. I feel sure they gathered at this place to take off on migration."

2008: Along the road to Wilmington, the woodlots are bare and brown. Light snow dulls the new winter wheat. When I arrived home at 4:30 this afternoon, I surprised a female ruby-crowned kinglet, a stubby, finch-like bird with a white eye ring, in the rose of Sharon bush in the front garden. She flicked her wings and peered at me, hopped over to the forsythia hedge. She was clearly on her way south to the Gulf from breeding grounds in Canada.

2009: Another soft morning in the 50s, misty rain off and on. One patch of gentle blue, surrounded by hazy clouds above me. The alley wet and bare, starlings whistling off to the east along Stafford Street, two starlings seen in Don's maple tree on Dayton Street. More and more honeysuckle leaves coming down leaving the hedge line empty. Limestone Street privets gradually turning violet gold. When I checked the white mulberry tree this afternoon, I saw almost all the remaining leaves had come down in the rain.

2011: The coldest morning so far, low in the mid 20s. The rest of the white mulberry foliage came down over night. The Osage leaves fluttering down, but many still hanging on.

2013: Returning from my walk with Bella this morning, I came upon a male cardinal attacking the reflecting windows on the camper I have parked on the street. So he is starting to defend his territory.

2014: The backyard snow is littered with the last Osage, redbud and river birch foliage after a vast Arctic intrusion, freezing temperatures all the way to the Gulf of Mexico.

2015: The Dayton Street beech and the Xenia Avenue sweet gums are three-fourths down, many ginkgoes in town still at half, Lil's burning bush still bright red. The newer Norway maples across the street keep maybe a third of their color. Buzzards circling the south end of town. Bob Barcus left a rambling poem-message about the roses still blooming in front of the bank downtown. Jill watched a large flock of starlings in the trees out side her window this afternoon. Heavy wind and rain this evening, a wet close to a mild and breezy day.

2016: Warm and sunny throughout the day, the high reaching 75 to tie the 1930 record. The koi were more active in the summer-like weather. Along the east border of the yard, bittersweet berries were opening to show their brighter seeds. The pussy willow buds above them were tight and ready for winter. Barometer dropping, prelude to real November wither. Downtown, the Zelcovas hold, and the post office pear tree is burnished gold and red, and shedding.

2017: Yesterday a walk before sunset along the bike path, the barometer falling, the sky just clear enough to provide glow to the olive green honeysuckle leaves and the burnished path sides and the second-spring water cress in the ditches. Winterberry vines hung along the path, red berries protruding from white shells. Sometimes we found bittersweet with its orange fruit holding all uncovered. We saw one coralberry bush with a few last, red-violet coralberries. A spinning cluster of craneflies followed us for a while across the old soybean field.

This morning a great murmuration of starlings came up from the southeast and circled and settled a few moments in the high Osage trees behind the house, then moved northwest. A squirrel chattered in the honeysuckles, and the wind grew harder. A robin whinnied twice near Dayton Street. The sparrows were skittish, fed sporadically in the early afternoon, then stayed away a long while, and then for a few minutes they swooped in to feed, then flew off in a whir, a flurry of beating wings, came back and forth twice and then were gone to hide from the restless weather like butterflies do in summer.

The wind came in crests and troughs, the sky pulling deep breaths in then pushing them out against the high trees, the sound of ocean waves landing ashore, the last leaves whirling away in handfuls and alone like moths. I rested in the silent pauses of the wave trains, became excited when the maples and locust trees rocked in the deepening swells, and the bamboo near my greenhouse bowed and rebounded over and over.

For hours the gray sky gave no hint of the change ahead. Then slowly the clouds became lower and darker, the afternoon turning to twilight. A formation of maybe two dozen Canadian geese suddenly appeared above me flying north. Then lightning and then thunder, then rain.

2020: All the white mulberry leaves are finally down. The Osage holds, as do some of the honeysuckle bushes on the north side of the yard.

2021: The foliage of Jill's red Japanese maple came apart in the night wind.

2022: Snow and deep cold settles in across the country. Several feet of lake-effect snow in Buffalo, New York. Large flock of boisterous geese at DeWine's Pond this morning.

Journal

Each place its own mind, its own psyche. Oak...Douglas fir...a certain scale to the topography, drenching rains in the winter, fog off-shore in the summer...all these together make up a particular state of mind, a place-specific intelligence shared by all the humans that dwell therein.... Each place its own psyche. each sky its own.

David Abram: *The Spell of the Sensuous*

There is an invisible but palpable grid that holds everything in order in this world. Everywhere you face, you face into the breath that emanates from a source of particular powers.

Peter London, *Drawing Closer to Nature*

From my window, I watch five maples across the way, curious about their geometry and the challenge of measuring this particular part of Earth and sky. I see the branches at hand, the perceived shapes of Lil's tree, Mrs. Timberlake's tree, Frank's tree, T.K.'s tree, the Danielsons' tree. (All of these people have passed to the other side, but their trees persist.)

Here, autumn has laid bare the secret grid. This is not my school geometry, but from my vantage point, I am entangled with right angles, equilateral triangles, scalene triangles, right triangles, radii, acute angles, pentagons, squares, parallelograms, rectangles, rhombuses, octagons, trapezoids, isosceles triangles, hexagons, obtuse angles.

All of those concepts and so many more fit with my trees, suggest a sort of topology in which nodes and links of their networks and enclosed spaces collude to create function.

Altogether, my High Street maples produce a full monty of Euclidian fantasy, their nudity hinting at the sense of deep space.

The window, like a great telescope, invites me to contemplate the topological geometry that lies before me, the arboreal Euclidian *Elements of the Maples in. the Yards of Lil, Frank, the Danielsons and Mrs. Timberlake,* Here I might intuit the mathematics and the astronomy of these maples, sort and name their constellations, number their leaves and be intimate with all their segments (and imagine the memories of their late guardians), and feel the grid and its power.

In quantum mechanics, "position" is like a strobe snapshot. Momentum is the life-created summation of many frames.

Robert Lanza, *Biocentrism*

If you didn't look just right,
you could miss them
moving slowly south,
one too-long leg after another.

When I heard them just after dawn
I thought I was hearing
turkeys in the woods,
not Sandhills on the beach.

But there they were,
out front,
no hurry to them,
snacking as they walked and rattling.

The beach was different from last year,
from two years ago,
different from when it was
a mile high river of ice.

But the cranes were the same:
visitors from before our world,
visitors you could have seen
if you stood still two million years ago,
and looked just right.

Jeff Crawford, "Look Just Right"

Sunrise/set: 7:24/5:16
Day's Length: 9 hours 52 minutes
Average High/Low: 49/33
Average Temperature: 41
Record High: 75 – 1930
Record Low: 12 – 1914

The Daily Weather

Today's highs: chances of 70s five percent, 60s thirty percent, 50s twenty percent, 40s thirty percent, 30s fifteen percent. Mornings below freezing occur about half the time. Rain occurs one day in four; snow is rare. The sun shines three quarters of the days.

The Natural Calendar

When next year's skunk cabbage pushes through the mud, summer still retains enough momentum to hold off early winter a little longer. Starlings are still gathering in the wood lots. Autumn violets and pansies can still be blooming. More than a third of the forsythia, silver olive, mock orange and honeysuckle hold on. The pears still have their leaves. Water striders still hunt in the sloughs this week. A few daddy longlegs are left in the old wood nettles and touch-me-nots. A few bees still come out, and moths emerge when the temperatures rise into the 60s.

When skunk cabbage appears, new winter wheat has turned fields bright green again. Lawns grow back; they can be long and thick beneath the fallen leaves. Garlic mustard is waiting for April all across the woodland floor. It sprouted fourteen months ago and has persevered with only a cluster of basal leaves all summer. In the swamp, colors deepen. Protected by the streams, watercress shines; dock and ragwort come back beside the dead field grasses.

With pasture growth slowed or stopped by the cold, many farmers feed hay to livestock. Throughout the northern half of the United States, fall tillage in field and garden, which often helps control insects and improve soil structure, ends before the onset of more inclement weather. Christmas trees have appeared at all the markets. In southeastern Ohio, residents begin to see migrating sandhill cranes flying toward the Gulf.

The early night sky of late November offers one the most spectacular stellar displays of the year, but it promises little warmth. Still, the stars are not fixed, and, in their movement, they become the most precise of allies.

An hour before sunrise, before the first color gives away the time of day, look south and imagine it is still evening instead of close to dawn. Then you'll see the sky has moved into its evening position for spring equinox. Eight hours – that is, four months in star time – from today's wintry evening message of Orion - all the signs of cold are setting in the west:

Regulus, centered overhead, announces the first bloom of violet cress and the full bloom of crocus. June's Arcturus is well up in the east calling out lilies. Warm Spica, the star of all the clovers, lies along the horizon. The Corona Borealis, crown of peonies and iris and lily-of-the-valley, rises nearby. Vega has come full circle, is guiding Deneb and the Swan back from the northeast, promising asters and goldenrod.

It is a matter of perspective. The morning sky is always four months ahead of the evening sky. Eight hours after you see November's Orion looming up to foretell winter, he is gone. In four hundred eighty minutes, eight hours, the stars have moved one hundred twenty days, deep into spring and summer.

Daybook

1982: Columbines are almost gone at the Cascades. Willows keep half their leaves. Water striders are still out. All oak leaves are down. Hepatica and ginger foliage is brown from frost. Wild onion is growing strong in the alleys. Winter wheat a couple of inches tall in the old cornfields – patches of emerald green in the otherwise beige landscape. Asparagus stalks have lost their summer color, now pale gold.

1983: On a warm, 65-degree day, starlings sing, two daddy longlegs lie together against the cedar siding on the west wall of the house. Geese fly over in the late afternoon. Birch and willow retain yellowing leaves. Catalpas are finally gone. Most raspberry leaves have withered. Motherwort still strong, comfrey has died back. A third of the Osage leaves are left. Most honeysuckles in the yard are bare, but in the woods they still hold on. The pussy willow by the back shed still has half its leaves.

1988: Starlings filled the morning trees. Geese went over the house three times today. First orange Christmas cactus bloomed.

1990: First aloe flower opened today in the greenhouse.

1995: Mild today after cold and snow. Craneflies spin in the afternoon sun. Starlings cluck in the trees. A cardinal sings off and on. I dug up one of the old strawberry beds for garlic planting.

1997: Crows pass through at 8:10 a.m., 2:20 p.m., 3:40 p.m. Osage leaves finally all came down today. Honeysuckles seven-eighths gone. At South Glen, time for tufts of ironweed and thimble plant, goldenrod, zigzag goldenrod, milkweed, cattails.

1999: Another perfect morning, mild, with high cirrus; the world here is so quiet, no birds, no crickets. This afternoon, one cardinal sang about 1:30. Starlings seen flocking at 3:30. In the Caribbean, a late hurricane, Lenny, moves in a strange once-in-a-century pattern from west to east, laying waste the central islands.

2001: My late yellow maple is finally shedding today. At school, all the white oaks are suddenly collapsing, one maybe nine-tenths gone, the other about two-thirds. With the rain and then frost, the high white mulberry leaves in the yard (which had held on longer than the lower leaves) floated down almost all at once. Ladybug at my window, one seen on the woodpile yesterday. Honeysuckle golden now across the farm landscape, a new season of gold, gift of the mild November. Silver olives thin out.

2004: A ginkgo on Dayton Street still holds its leaves, and the Dayton-Street beech is still full gold. Downtown, the pear foliage is red and starting to thin. The sweet gum across the street holds at maybe a fifth. Mild days continue to grace this November.

2008: Ice formed on the pond overnight. In the alley this gray, cold morning, robins were peeping all around me, and by Mrs. Timberlake's yard, I saw the first two juncos of the season. In the back yard (and in front of the library) the oak-leaf hydrangeas are deep red and chocolate brown and green. Yesterday, the Osage leaves were falling heavily, and today they continue to clatter through their branches, piling up around the shed, deep golden. They will all be down tonight, just like in 1997.

2009: One pink tea rose has bloomed this week, and many of the

Knockout roses have buds or old blossoms. First coralberries noticed. Forsythia is thinning quickly, golden-violet. Osage fruits along High Street are becoming pale yellow, losing their earlier chartreuse tint. In the alley, the thin-leaved coneflower holds on. One robin seen sitting on a fencepost behind Mrs. Timberlake's yard. One crow flew over when I was feeding the birds, one buzzard as I was coming back from the walk with Bella.

2011: Liz reports Jenny saw the first flock of sandhill cranes flying over the south edge of town around 1:00 p.m. today. (This is the earliest sighting as of 2016. Jon Whitmore heard what were probably cranes on November 7 of 2017).

2012: Sunny and mild today, starlings chattering throughout the morning, a robin seen next to the pond, a pair of blue jays and several chickadees taking turns at the back feeders, and a cardinal singing and singing while I put up snow guards on the roof around 2:30 in the afternoon. A young male cardinal has been attacking the mirror-like finish of the camper window over and over, all day long, for several days now. In the back yard, the last leaf has finally fallen from the last blueberry bush.

2014: The last two nights of deep cold have put an end to the season of autumn leaf fall. Only a few pears and beeches hold out. Along Lake Erie in western New York, amazing snowfalls of over six feet.

2015: Netting removed from over the pond, both filters cleaned out, chemical added to help clear the water. Fish very sluggish and reluctant to rise.

2016: Netting remains on the pond: The Chinese elm and the pink quince still have most of their foliage, but eaves are starting to come down more rapidly on the white mulberry as the first real cold spell of the autumn moves through. The New England aster plants have turned dusky ochre, their round, gray seed heads soft and tufted. The first Christmas cactus blossoms (white-pink) have opened. And there was snow for a few minutes in the early afternoon.

2017: Last night's storm pulled off almost all the quince leaves. Lil's burning bush is bare. The Japanese maple has thinned considerably. The Osage and Jeanie's redbud and the lilacs still hold, their leaves stiff and brown, the Dayton Street beech and the Zelcovas downtown are still quite full, rusty brown. In the greenhouse, the old Christmas cacti are in early bloom.

2019: With Ranger this morning, no birdsong until 7:10. Then, one cardinal song south of where I was walking, then the crows woke up. Lil's burning bush still holds.

2020: Ellis Pond at a pink and azure and golden sunset, warm 50s, new moon in the east, and a great flock of geese circled the soybean fields, settled in, rose again, circled, settled in, rose again and then returned to the pasture area for the night. Now the ash and maple groves are completely bare, their branches black and pure against sky.

2021: More and more tattering of the remaining trees. Burning bush shrubs are shedding more now, late, bright yellow sugar maples coming apart, zelcovas thinning quickly, the Dayton Street birch and pear trees solid burnished, rusty still, the white mulberry and the Osage still keep their leaves. Reading back over the years, I note that there have been no starlings in the neighborhood this entire fall. I miss them. News reports through the summer indicated that starlings were among the birds most affected by the unnamed virus that was sweeping the nation, Ohio one of the hardest hit.

2022: Two nights in the 20s, and almost all the Osage leaves came down, the lawn golden, the tree about bare. Like today in 1997 and 2008. Wind and sun throughout the day. Three very large murmurations of starlings seen near sundown on the way to and from Fairborn. h

2023: A crisp morning with fog and frost and then bright sun, and the season seemed to have suddenly shifted in the night from Middle Fall to Late Fall, even though the white mulberry leaves and the Osage leaves. have not all come down, the yard seems more naked, the air sharper and more aggressive. Still, walking downtown, I heard robins peeping. This evenng, Maria, Barbara's daughter. notified me that her mother died tody. A loyal correspondent and the best of long-distance freinds whom I will miss greatly.

From"Crosing April" by Barbara Valdez

,

The student and lover of nature has this advantage over people who gad up and down the world, seeking some novelty or excitement; he has only to stay at home and see the procession pass. The great globe swings around to him like a revolving showcase; the change of the seasons is like the passage of strange and new countries; the zones of the earth, with all their beauties and marvels, pass one's door, and linger long in the passing.

John Burroughs

Sunrise/set: 7:25/5:16
Day's Length: 9 hours 51 minutes
Average High/Low: 48/32
Average Temperature: 40
Record High: 73 – 1931
Record Low: 11 – 1914

The Daily Weather

Chances of snow are 15 percent, for rain 35 percent, and the sun breaks through just 50 percent of the days. Highs are in the mild 60s on 30 percent of the afternoons, in the 50s twenty percent of the time, in the 40s twenty-five percent and in the 30s another 25 percent. Low temperatures remain above freezing half of the nights.

The Natural Calendar

Nature! Great parent! Whose unceasing hand
Rolls round the seasons of the changeful year.

James Thomson

Now Winter Wheat Greening Season greens the fields as Bluebird Migrating Season and Cricketsong Season close. On the high wires, Sparrow Hawk Season arrives. Bittersweet Fruit Dropping Season comes to the bittersweet vines, and Decorative Pear Leafturn Season transforms city streets. In the greenhouse, it is Aloe Flowering Season and Christmas Cactus Flower Season.

Along the West Coast, this week brings the annual Crab Harvest Season. Crawdad Season starts in Louisiana, crawdads moving into flooded rice fields to feed on the remnants of that crop.

Daybook

1982: Despite all the cold, mums are still bright. Mallow, one pansy, some parsley, petunias, calendulas, alyssum, chard, broccoli, chives hold, too; the kale is even growing a few new leaves. The roadside grass is mostly brown now, only patches of green. Seed heads of Queen Anne's lace bow to the ground. All but a handful of leaves gone from the tall Osage in back, and the mock orange and the pussy willow. Some forsythia bushes almost bare, others have half their leaves. Privets are still solid, but their leaves are a yellow-gray-green.

1983: Bee flying around in church this morning. Large fly in the house. On a drive into Dayton, I saw maples with more than half their foliage, also poplars. There was a marked difference between the partially clad city and the bare countryside.

1984: Petunias, calendula, alyssum, pansy survive 18-degree freeze this morning.

1988: Raspberry and black raspberry leaves almost all gone, also mock orange. Some honeysuckle branches are bare, red berries thick. All the pear foliage on Xenia Avenue has come down in maybe five days. A few sweet gum leaves, yellow and red, holding. The yard grass is bright green like the pastures and winter wheat. Squirrels chatter in the morning, few other birds. Tornadoes out of season destroyed towns in the South yesterday, and a week or so ago.

1989: Cardinal sings at dawn.

1990: South Glen: Bluebirds – the last flock coming through?

1991: Road kills increase in the mild, wet weather: three opossums in three days, rare this late in the month.

1992: South Glen, sun, middle 60s: Ironweed seeds half gone. At Far Hole, all the Osage fruits and leaves are down. A cardinal singing on the other side of the woods off and on through my walk. Loud calls of a pileated woodpecker. At the river's edge, the water is rippled blue, black, green and brown, tree branches tangled in reflections. One bluebird sighted. A tan moth, maybe an inch in wingspan fluttered from one clump of leaves to another, almost like a grasshopper. Three dandelions seen along the way; they are like overwintering robins, stragglers showing up through the fall. One burst milkweed pod, silk dangling. At High Prairie: a field of goldenrod seeds covered with dew shining in the sun, fruit far more exotic than its flowers. A few small oaks hold here, chocolate brown. Moss has new sprouts on an old log. Banks of box elder seeds shimmering. Most wingstem seeds hold, but all are fragile. Burdock burs hold, strong. All but one or two shriveled staghorns are gone from the sumac, thistles bedraggled, most undone, scattered, foliage curled and shrunken like dried seaweed. Small brown spider in the leaves. Thimble plant unraveling. In the front garden, more crocus planted.

1995: After a very cold few weeks, the sun is shining, the temperature up into the low 50s. On the way home from Wilberforce, I saw three orange and black woolly-bear caterpillars crossing the road – today is the latest I've ever seen them. I planted the garlic patch this afternoon, about 150 square feet of space. Jeanie reports the crows are congregating west of Springfield, the earliest we've noticed them arrive.

1996: November's beauty is the first of April's, green of last leaves shining, the first leaves of the year. Sweet rocket high and bushy, hemlock strong and tall, chickweed spreading.

1999: The New England aster leaves have yellowed, and some of their seed heads are tufting. A few poplar and lilac leaves hold on in the south border. The cold front of the 19th passed through last night, this morning clear and serene. First birdseed (thistles) put out today.

2000: All the white mulberry leaves are down. Ginkgo finally gone at school. Ice on the pond.

2001: People ask me about why I give the moons different names in my almanacks, but a person's own steps and phases could be named according to the visible or invisible landscape, like named moons, guiding each observer in private seasons. If there is little difference between the mind and what it sees, then the creatures of the world and their names in our mindfulness become both cause and effect, impeccably binding us together in a strange stability of ephemeral beauty, passage, birth and death.

2002: Lil's maple leaves have all withered, but many remain on their branches. Jerry and Lee's sweet gum is bright yellow. In the south garden, one stella d'oro lily blooming. Two yellow roses and one pink achillea are open in the north garden.

2003: Jerry and Lee's sweet gum has lost almost all its foliage but is still one of the few trees along High Street to have any leaves at all. In the north garden along the wall, the purple scabiosa has withstood the hard freezes to outlast all the other summer flowers.

2004: Fragments of burning bush foliage remain here and there.

2007: Ginkgo leaves collapsed on Rachel's tree two days ago; the larger ginkgoes along Xenia Avenue are about half down today. Red-gold pear, sweet gum and oak foliage is prominent throughout town and south into Wilmington. I saw a large flock of blackbirds or grackles yesterday on the way to Cedarville.

2009: Rachel's ginkgo and all the others in town have been bare for at least ten days. This morning has been quiet: clouds at four this morning, then clearing suddenly, Orion in the west, Gemini above, the Dipper deep south of Polaris. Now a hazy peach sunrise.

2010: I got up late this morning, after 6:00, and Venus was well up over the Danielsons' house into the empty branches of their maple. Jeanie's young river birch in the back yard is down to just a small fraction of its leaves (while the birches near the shopping center have been bare for weeks), and the honeysuckles are dwindling quickly, berries more prominent now than their yellow leaves. The Osage foliage has started to come down here, but our tree is far more stubborn than those along the river.

2012: Yellow Springs to Madison, Wisconsin: The backyard river birch has only a skeleton of leaves this morning. The sky cloudless, dusky haze throughout most of the trip. I passed through areas of fog twice in the plains of Illinois, and wispy cirrus appeared as I approached Wisconsin. The landscape uniform throughout, all the fields but one cut over.

Willow trees – which still held their brown-green leaves in Ohio had lost most of their foliage by the time I reached northern Illinois. Three white-breasted hawks seen along the way, but only one sizeable flock of starlings, other small flocks on high wires. The weather was mild, and I drove with the heat off, my jacket off, and the windows open for hundreds of miles. The roadside grasses became browner the further north I drove, but hemlock was bushy in patches throughout the trip.

2013: Jeanie's river birch is bare except for a few shriveled leaves that hold on. Two brown leaves left on the blueberry bush. I planted crocus in the dooryard garden late this afternoon. Winter wheat showing in rows in fields between here and Columbus. Neysa and I ate supper at the Sunrise Café, a housefly that had escaped from the cold visited our booth.

2015: Robins still peeping in the morning. Winter storm "Bella" sweeps across the Plains and Midwest.

2016: The Dayton Street beech is full rust gold, the Xenia Avenue ginkgoes are mostly down, the Zelcovas on the way out of town rich red brown. Lil's maple, the backyard white mulberry and the Osage are at about half. Jeanie's river birch keeps a delicate scattering of golden leaves. A new winter storm threatens the Northeast.

2017: Under the waning moon, the Thanksgiving week ahead is expected to be cold but not stormy. At Ellis Pond, the swamp chestnut oak, the shingle oak and the red oaks held their chocolate brown leaves. Vern Hogans' English oak was still olive green and fully leafed, as was the sawtooth oak. The yellow poplar still kept its foliage, shriveled, and its calices spilled wispy seeds when I touched them. The weeping willow was bare, the cypresses about nine-tenths down. I saw farmers harvesting corn as I drove back from Beavercreek.

2018: North to Wisconsin: One large murmuration of starlings, four smaller flocks. Three hawks, three road kills. I take notes, thinking that these 500 miles might show no creatures at all in a few years, gone like the insects on the windshield.

2019: Lil's tree still holds at about a fourth, foliage brown. Robins heard peeping near Stafford Street this morning, and a small flock chirping as they travelled through the high trees of the ash grove.

2020: A warm 61 degrees this afternoon. I took the netting from the koi pond, cleaned out the pump and washed the lower south windows. At sundown near the Glass Farm wetlands, the ghostly intermittent call of a tree frog. A dozen ducks on the water, occasional quacks.

2022: Low in the teens this morning, the coldest so far since last winter. Neysa reports a sudden turning of the leaves in Campello, Italy, the latest she remembers it.

Journal: Hiding

As the last leaves of the year come down, seed catalogs arrive in my mailbox, and I plan for May under the Bedding Plant Moon. Usually, I order a few packages of geraniums, coleus and petunias, and I start them under grow lights close to the furnace, which happens to be in the attic.

If I keep the soil warm, moist and close enough to the fluorescent bulbs, the seeds germinate within a week or so and then develop steadily throughout the winter.

Although I enjoy the flowers that the plants produce in spring and summer, for me, the best part of sprouting seeds in winter is sitting next to them, feeling safe and disconnected from the snow and from the rest of my life.

There, the only sound is the low purr of the furnace fan. All around me and the plants and the soft lights, the space is dark and private. The smell of new earth thins the musty smell of the attic. I hide, shielded by a comforter that is part childhood, part angel.

It seems that my eyes and my longing itself search the magical glowing green of the sprouts for meaning. All their prophetic power rests in their two or four leaves, all of their potential compressed into the most delicate and vulnerable flesh.

Here there is no thought of maturity or harvest, no logical conclusion, no socially redeeming value, no death. I do not think about the eventual work of transplanting and mulching, conflicts with insects and weather and blights. Even the promise of beauty, color and fragrance is irrelevant. Only the coverlet of this time in this place with these creatures makes sense.

Thus times do shift; each thing his turn does hold;
New things succeed as former things grow old.

Robert Herrick

November 21st
The 325th Day of the Year

The leaves are all dead on the ground
Save those the oak is keeping
To ravel them one by one
And let them go scraping and creeping
Out over the crusted snow,
When others are sleeping.

Robert Frost

Sunrise/set: 7:27/5:15
Day's Length: 9 hours, 48 minutes
Average High/Low: 48/32
Average Temperature: 40
Record High: 75 – 1934
Record Low: 12 – 1964

The Daily Weather

Chances of rain today are 30 percent, for snow five percent. Clouds give way to partly clear conditions more than half of the time. Highs reach the 60s on 15 percent of the days, are in the 50s on 25 percent, in the 40s on 30 percent, the 30s on 25 percent, and only in the 20s on five percent of the afternoons. Nights below freezing come six years in a decade.

The Natural Calendar

The final rites of fall include a chronology of the last leaves and fruits. Major losses occur on beeches and pears as autumn ends. Sometimes oaks are the holdouts, sometimes forsythia or a hardy honeysuckle. Sometimes sweet gums and poplars keep a few leaves this late in the year; sometimes protected oak-leaf hydrangeas, Osage, mock orange or lilacs outlast all the other trees and shrubs.

Daybook

1982: Bradford pears on Xenia Avenue still have their foliage, rusty red. Small sugar maples by the old Carr greenhouse at the

171

end of High Street still have their leaves, dull gold.

1983: South Glen at sunset: Cardinals, doves, downy woodpeckers in the trees. All the leaves are gone except a few honeysuckles. Ginger, parsnip, nettle burned by the frost. Crane flies spinning through the black wingstem and the tufted goldenrod, catching the light of the orange sun.

1985: The leaves all fell at once today from the new pecan tree.

1986: Starlings seem to have left town. They had been eating crab apples just a week ago. I took them for granted. I did hear a bobwhite calling, but the silence of winter seems to be setting in. A few honeysuckle leaves and berries left. No violets seen blooming in the woods. Rivers high but clear.

1990: Red crab apple fruit prominent along Dayton Street now. Bluebirds seen at South Glen, and the pear leaves begin to fall on Xenia Avenue. One cardinal song at 2:00 p.m.

1993: Robins gone at South Glen, but an occasional call heard in town today. Yellow Osage leaves came down in the light wind today.

1997: The beech tree on Dayton Street is losing its golden brown leaves now.

1998: Gerry writes from Florida: "You asked what flowers are blooming. Besides orchids? Many many. The bougainvilleas (local Spanish spelling) are in full bloom (as they are almost year round); the pond lilies are just about to bloom; the tababulia trees have buds and will bloom in about a month... and there are so many more.... Are the citrus ripening? Yes, my regular stock are -- ruby red grapefruit almost ready, and in another two weeks my mandarin and navel oranges will be ready and then in full production for three to four months. Some growers manage to put out citrus stock around the year, right through the summer heat, too. Then there's fruit like my mango and avocado that produce in mid-late summer. I need to plant my radish and lettuce this week since this is the time for tender vegetables that will be harvestable in January and February."

1999: In meditation class, the teacher told me told to follow the spaces between the sounds I heard. Now, in late November I might do just as well to follow the spaces between summer and winter. The windows look out onto the new geometry of the mulberry and the walnut branches. The openings define their borders. The black street comes into the yard again, the hermitage barrier of forsythia and honeysuckles thinned. The sounds of the cars (and the sounds of time between the cars) are unfiltered by foliage. I can see the edges of the rocks at the bottom of the pond now. The water hyacinths are gone. Pickerel plants and arrowhead plants, purple loosestrife, wild flag, water willow, water lily have all thinned to stalks, uncovering the fish. I haven't raked the grass; green shows through, widens as the leaves decay. The flowers and weeds have died back in the garden, revealing the soil again. The giant leaves of the great blue hosta plant have shriveled like snake skin. The gray fruit disappears from the New England asters, and their shiny calyces emerge. The phlox plants are empty, their pointed, lanky sepals curling.

2000: While I ate lunch in the truck with Buttercup, I watched a flock of finches working the sweet gum tree fruits, digging out the seeds from their hollows. Below them, juncos fed on what the finches lost.

2001: Sycamores in Columbus mostly down, pears shedding in Xenia, chestnuts three-fourths bare, Susi's late maple gone, most of the land in central Ohio plowed.

2003: I saw a small flock of vultures circling low over Grinnell Road on my way back from walking with Mike this morning. The temperature reached 60 degrees this afternoon. A fly was buzzing in the work shed.

2004: Crows call at 7:15 this morning. Betty Ross from the Raptor Center said she had seen a flock of crows attacking a black vulture last week. She added that crows never attack turkey vultures – and that black vultures haven't been in this area until just the last year or two.

2006: Jerry and Lee's sweet gum has lost almost all its leaves. Sundog seen in the west over Dayton this afternoon at 4:15.

2007: To Madison, Wisconsin today, beginning at 67 degrees, driving through hard rain for several hundred miles, ending in heavy snow and wind. A few hawks seen, a few small flocks of starlings. We left behind many pears, beeches, oaks, and even late maples with foliage, entering a countryside that became more and more empty the further past Indianapolis (the further above the 40th Parallel) we drove. All but the broad-leafed Norway maples had fallen in Wisconsin. One burning bush had collapsed maybe a day or so before our arrival.

2008: Deep cold in the teens this morning, clear skies, waning moon. When I walked the alley, a few robins peeped and whinnied, small groups of starlings sat in the bare trees whistling and chirping. The leaves on Frank's silver maple tree have all shriveled, but hold. On Dayton Street, the beech is about half down.

2010: Crows boisterous when I went to get wood this morning around 8:00. I remembered what they said: We are not alone; the world is well fashioned.

2011: A cardinal sang at 8:30 this morning when I was walking down Limestone Street with Bella. A robin was peeping in the alley.

2012: Madison, Wisconsin: Crows here at 6:52, about the same time they would be calling in Yellow Springs. A steady south wind blowing today, temperature forecast to be in the 60s, one of the warmest Thanksgivings in my memory.

2013: More crocus planted in the dooryard garden, the tips of snowdrops protruding here and there when the mulch is moved away. Near the street, wild grapes fall to the sidewalk like the honeysuckle berries, staining the cement like red and black mulberries.

2014: Casey called this sunny, crisp day: At about 10:20 in the morning," he said, "I heard sandhill cranes. They were heading south-southeast and were too far away to count. They sure were making a racket, though!" Then Casey called again two hours later. He had seen another herd of what he thought was fifty or sixty sandhills. "It was a gorgeous sight!" And then Dianne sent a note at 12:56: "Just a few minutes ago a flock of sandhills flew over my house. Lovely sight against the blue sky. Definitely not geese. Whiter and making clear crane noises. What fun to see." And so these were sightings of two or possibly three waves of cranes riding the huge high-pressure system that has been coming across Ohio from the northwest for over a week. They were the second-earliest sightings in my records. Liz's on the 19th in 2011 was the earliest.

2016: A robin whinny near Jill's house just after dawn. Most ginkgoes completely down. Zelcovas and sweet gums still quite colorful. The first fallen sweet gum seed balls noticed near Greene Street, and the first bittersweet hulls on the front sidewalk. Peggy's burning bush and so many others in town keep their deep red, highlighting the November hedges.

2020: A few weeks ago I was walking Bella, our border collie, through the alley around a quarter after nine in the morning. The maples had lost their leaves by then, the hackberries and oaks half down. I could hear starlings and grackles ahead of me to the north, and I hurried down to see them.

Past the apple tree, I came under the cries and the rushing of the great flock. They knew where they were going: southeast, stopping in the branches above me for a just few seconds, calling to one another, looking out above the high canopy, then hurrying, diving on, one after another,

I was swept away and then held tight in their direction and their certainty. They covered me up, it seemed, in their numbers. Their whirring, chortling migration filled the space between the street and the silver maple where I stood.

The tent of this flock's passage was such a safe place against the cold ahead. The coverlet was force enough, fortification against what would surely come, filtering and sorting through, in just this instant in the alley, the daunting approach of the winter, and giving me a balance like the birds themselves must have felt, pulled by time and context out into the autumn sky.

Surrounded, I had no place left to turn: the starlings and the grackles had taken all the options. I stood loved, cradled, suspended, caressed, enfolded in a blanket of pinions, here on this familiar ground, in the presence of the white asters with red centers and the violet asters with arrowhead leaves.

2021: Late holdings on several Xenia Avenue ginkgoes and sweet gums. Zelcovas thinning now. The white mulberry and the Osage at home keep their foliage.

2023: Departure for Madison, Wisconsin. The shades of green projected by the honeysuckle and the roadside grasses all fade to gray and brown above Bloomington, Illinois. Some oaks and rusty foliage of sweet gums kept a hint of Late Fall in the landscape. No hawks seen, only a handful of flocking birds.

> *Tonight the winds begin to rise*
> *and roar from yonder dripping day.*
> *The last red leaf is whirled away,*
> *The rooks are blown about the skies.*

Alfred Lord Tennyson

November 22nd
The 326th Day of the Year

Now bright in the golden stars stands Sagittarius
And thrusts the Scorpion with his bended bow.

Ovid

Sunrise/set: 7:28/5:14
Day's Length: 9 hours 46 minutes
Average High/Low: 48/32
Average Temperature: 40
Record High: 74 – 1900
Record Low: 8 – 1964

The Daily Weather

Highs in the 60s come ten percent of the afternoons. Fifties occur 40 percent of the time, 40s thirty percent of the time, 30s twenty percent. Half the days are cloudy, and half are partly sunny. Rain falls one day out of three, but snow almost never comes to Yellow Springs on this date.

The Weather in the Week Ahead

The third week of Late Fall, is typically a stark and windy week that marks the decline of average highs below 50 degrees throughout the region, and the end to any reasonable chance of a day above 70. Nights below zero even become possible now. The sixth cold front of the month, arriving around the 24th, often brings rain on the 23rd (there is a 50 percent chance of that). The seventh high-pressure system generally arrives on November 28th, preceded by rain 70 percent of the time on the 27th, that date being the wettest day in the month's weather history. November 28th, 29th, and 30th have the best odds of the month for snow. After the 25th, the percentage of cloudy days almost doubles over the average for the rest of November.

The Natural Calendar

All but a few shriveled staghorns have fallen from the sumac. Thistles are bedraggled, foliage curled. Fields of dry goldenrod heads glow in the sun, more exotic than when they were in flower. Red and orange berries are unveiled by the end of leaf-fall on the bittersweet and the hawthorns.

New England aster and stonecrop foliage turned yellow in early November; now the plants are shedding. Unprotected garden lettuce and the autumn growth of rhubarb have usually withered. Hosta leaves have collapsed into the remnants of maples, ginkgoes and white mulberries. Beside all of the decay, large patches of dandelions come into bloom, marking a final fanfare of second spring.

The day becomes shorter by seven minutes during the week ahead, the last time this year that the day loses so much time along the 40th Parallel. Sunset is within just a few minutes of the earliest of the year when the sun comes into Sagittarius; it will remain close to its earliest time until the second week of December, when it starts to set later in the evening.

Two hours before midnight, the sky carries the forms of early winter: the Pleiades, Taurus and Orion are rising, the Milky Way cuts across the sky from east to west, Andromeda lies directly over Yellow Springs, and the Summer Triangle is setting over Dayton.

Daybook

1982: Tan moth fluttering in the twilight by the garden wall.

1983: Clifton Gorge: Viburnum thinning. Fat blackberry canes only have a few red-orange leaves. Hepatica leaves are purple from the frost. Some small sedum is growing back on the woods floor. A flock of geese went over at 3:15 this afternoon, pointed south. Red staghorns still hold here, still red.

1985: All the Dayton Street beech leaves are down.

1986: Cardinal sings off and on all morning.

1988: Sparrows chattering. Their conversations seem louder than in the summer, and more like spring territorial and mating disputes. Paperwhites started today, two inches protruding.

1989: Cardinal sings at 7:14, fourteen minutes before sunrise. Starlings in my ginkgo all day cackling. Aloe has almost completed its blooming in the greenhouse.

1992: Aloe about finished flowering in the greenhouse.

1994: First sparrow hawk of the year seen diving into the grass along the freeway. Around Springfield, the crows are everywhere.

1999: Along the bike path, the garlic mustard fills the ditches, sweet rocket foliage is fat here and there, soft mullein plants spread their basal leaves, hemlock is lush and bushy. In town, there are still some yellow mums. In the greenhouse, the first winter tomatoes are ripening. On the way to Dayton, I saw one yard full of dandelion heads gone to seed, an April sight. All through the city streets, the pears are coming down, the beeches too (here in Yellow Springs, the beech on Dayton Street seven-eighths down). Honeysuckles are still yellow green and thinning, accentuating the fresh grass with their spring-like glow. In the afternoon, I mowed the lawn for the last time, mulched the leaves into the ground. The smell was an April and May smell. Birds were at the feeder: three chickadees, a pair of wrens, a purple finch. Geese flew over town in a long line maybe half an hour past sundown; it was just light enough to see them. The newspaper reported wild turkeys wandering through yards, "escaping from the Thanksgiving hunt." This is the first time I've heard of the wild turkeys making it into town since they were planted here a decade or so ago well downstream from Yellow Springs.

2000: Sparrow hawk seen on the way to Fairborn.

2001: North to Wisconsin: Willows yellow at Indianapolis. Grass mixed, tan to green like late March. Some lawns, pastures bright. Silver olives down, fragments like glitter, specs of pale green. Fields alternating rusty tan to brown, to shades of beige. Flock of gulls in a cornfield.

2002: I found a woolly-bear caterpillar crawling along on the living room rug this evening.

2003: A cardinal and a wren sang at 7:01 this morning. Then silence. Lee and Jerry's sweet gum is down to maybe a fifth of its leaves. Mild 60s today – an Asian lady beetle landed on the back door as I came in from the yard. A mosquito flew around me this evening when I was watching television.

2004: The beech on Dayton Street is deep rust. Jerry and Lee's sweet gum has lost all but maybe five to ten percent of its leaves. Downtown, and all along Xenia Avenue, the pear trees are red and gold; shedding has begun. In Washington Court House, dandelion seed heads are common in the field across from school, the warm weather of the past week having brought a surge in flowering.

2006: This morning as I was reading by the fire, a medium-sized camel cricket came walking by and proceeded to go under the wood stove. The Osage leaves have come down in the last week; the forsythia, lilac and mock orange foliage is almost gone. The New England aster seed heads are all puffy and silver. I worked outside stacking scrap wood by the rose of Sharon hedge, was covered with a shower of fuzzy seeds when I bumped the branches. At the north end of the brick patio, another of the crocus we planted in September has bloomed, a purple one, fat, an inch or so across.

2007: Tat told me that her juncos stay the summer in Madison, only two hundred miles north of Yellow Springs. By her bird feeders, a witch hazel keeps its bright flowers in spite of the hard freeze.

2008: Most of the winterberries are bursting their hulls in the alley, falling to the ground. Two overwintering robins on my morning walk, one of them roosting on a bent branch of Mateo's red mulberry tree, the other on the fence behind the Danielsons'. Hard frost has withered almost all the remaining leaves.

2010: Mild in the 70s today with sun and clouds and wind. Heavy leaf fall from the Zelkova and the decorative pear trees. Over the past week, the Dayton Street beech has lost all of its middle and high leaves, is down to maybe a tenth of its foliage. Half a dozen dandelions in bloom on the north side of Limestone Street. A medium-sized camelback cricket got trapped in the bathtub this afternoon. Full moon tonight, storms across the North, rain forecast for early morning, cold for tomorrow.

2013: Two mild days of rain: this morning the koi are looking for food, race around the pond when they see me coming. Zelcovas are mostly bare now. Gusts of wind brought down Peggy's pear leaves when I walked by. I planted the remaining crocus and aconites before dark.

2016: To Madison, Wisconsin once again: Hard and cold south wind all the way, dramatic cloud formations, numerous fat murmurations of starlings throughout, trees thinning to bare along the highways, but in Madison, the change is not so extreme, the red burning bush leaves still hold at half.

2017: Madison, Wisconsin: A mild Thanksgiving after a chilly and windy drive here on the 20th. Few changes between Wisconsin and Ohio. A large flock of seagulls in a field in western Ohio, but no murmurations or hawks seen on the way north. John Blakelock called from Yellow Springs to say he had a greenbrier vine and a rhododendron with blossoms.

2018: Madison, Wisconsin: Occasional robin clucking heard as I walked Santi, Tat's dog.

2020: Judy reports from Goshen, Indiana, 200 miles northwest of Yellow Springs: She and bill saw hundreds of gulls at Fiddler's Pond yesterday. Jill and I saw a long flock of starlings this afternoon as we walked home along Dayton Street.

2021: Under early Sagittarius, the third week of Late Fall is the most porous, maybe the most mysterious time of the season, the most suggestive of both the future completion of leaf drop and also of the past memorabilia of September and October.

The recent snows created temporary openings in remaining foliage, hiding and highlighting decay in misty collages of dangling fragments, masking black tree trunks from the undergrowth, absences becoming fill between branches, snowflakes on the seed heads of virgin's bower and asters: elaboration of tufts.

Fog blended and blurred what was left of the crisp rust of late zelcovas and beeches. Bare trees seemed more distant because of the snow, space dictated by appearance. Gusts of wind swirled murmurations of flurries against the tallest oaks that had kept their leaves. Buildup of the snow on hedges of Japanese honeysuckle and forsythia, settled into mounds, prophesy of great winter piles and drifts.

Bittersweet and euonymus fruits disappeared into the frozen coverlet. Yellow witch hazel flowers pulled in, shriveling; Hosta leaves collapsed into the remnants of maples, ginkgoes and mulberries. Haze created hollows in old garden plantings, keeping me at bay with external cataracts that made dusky barriers to the other side of December.

The fields are cold at Jacoby swamp,
Brambles tangled in thistles and milkweed,
Blackberries gone to jam and brandy.

Leon Quel

November 23rd
The 327th Day of the Year

The winter wren is back, quick
Among the tree roots by the stream,
Feeding from stem to stone to stick,
And in his late return the rhyme
Of years again completes itself.

Wendell Berry

Sunrise/set: 7:29/5:14
Day's Length: 9 hours 45 minutes
Average High/Low: 47/31
Average Temperature: 39
Record High: 72 – 1931
Record Low: 13 – 1970

The Daily Weather

Today's high temperature distribution: 60s on ten percent of the days, 50s on 30 percent, 40s on 45 percent, 30s on 15 percent. Skies are overcast two days out of three; rain falls half the time, and snow is unlikely. For the first time since March 20th, average low temperatures fall below freezing.

The Natural Calendar

By November 23, the sun enters the Early Winter sign of Sagittarius. My notes from the day offer a thin composite of impressions for that transition in Yellow Springs. Like most of the days this week, the 23rd is a narrative of migrating blackbirds, restless geese, the gathering of crows in the fields north of town, the continued shedding of the red-gold pear leaves and the sienna beeches, the flowering of witch hazel, the collapse of bittersweet pods. Sometimes it is like a soft September day, sometimes one of hard frost, sometimes a day on which sandhill cranes, forecasting the last cold wave of the month, pass above Yellow Springs.

1984: Forsythia bushes hold at half. Beech leaves start to fall. In Wisconsin, willow leaves persist, yellow-green.

1985: Geese fly over 7:54 a.m. Doves, juncos, a blue jay, and a cardinal join the sparrows at the feeder.

1989: Downtown pear foliage still red and full. Geese fly back and forth every day. The red-orange Christmas cactus is in full bloom, the white maybe a fourth.

1992: First junco at the feeder, another tan finch too, cardinal singing for a while at 8:00 this morning. Mock orange, lilac almost all gone, forsythia more than half fallen. Downtown pears hold at maybe two-thirds. Housefly in the greenhouse. Red-orange Christmas cactus full bloom, and the white one has five flowers open.

1994: Finally, three days before breaking a record, Yellow Springs experienced its first hard freeze of the fall, temperatures into the 20s. Many of the white mulberry leaves and the Osage near the shed held on until last night, then with the cold, they all were down by morning.

1995: To Chicago: the trees bare throughout, even the willows and most of the oaks. No forsythia, only a few honeysuckle leaves left. Scattered flocks of pigeons and crows, a few geese, cross over the highway.

1997: Walking downtown, blustery afternoon, clouds and sun, wind from the northwest. Forsythia leaves were thinning, but one bush on Limestone Street was almost in full bloom (our bushes only had a single branch with blossoms). Up Dayton Street, the witch hazel was still in flower. Bittersweet berries holding along the sidewalk.

1999: First almost ripe tomatoes discovered at the west end of the greenhouse. They had been hidden by a red geranium. Outside it's so warm that I have the back door open. I can hear the crows west of town. These are the shortest days of the year, twenty minutes from solstice, but there is so much sun and light it seems like summer. A cabbage butterfly looking for nectar in the South Garden at 1:45 this afternoon, the latest in the year I've ever seen one. A yellow jacket reported in town. Late this afternoon, I came across a long flock of blackbirds, perhaps a mile in length, following the freeway south.

2000: Crows at 7:11 a.m. Hosta leaves finally collapse after nights in the teens and twenties. Osage holds but burned.

2003: A cardinal at 7:04 a.m., sky partly cloudy, temperature in the 50s. Pear trees have most of their leaves, red and yellow, along Xenia Avenue. The Dayton Street beech only has its lower foliage, golden.

2004: Cardinals singing off and on throughout the morning, the skies gray, temperature mild in the 50s. Greg called this evening: he's still watching the skunks come to his bird feeder.

2006: By today, almost all of the pale hulls of the bittersweet have fallen, leaving the bright orange berries.

2007: Jeanie and I went to my sister Tat's house for a family get-together in Wisconsin, and we arrived the night before Thanksgiving just as the wind picked up and rain turned to heavy flakes of snow. By morning, the sky was clear and the air was sharp. The ground and rooftops were white, all the leaves down and covered from the storm.

Before breakfast, I went walking with Bella, our border collie. The sun had come up an hour before, and it was shining through the bare trees. Crows were calling from the bike path behind my sister's house, a house that was only two blocks from where our parents had moved in the early 1960s.

I walked down the quiet Madison backstreet, surrounded by a sense of being completely at home. Something in the way the wind blew, some familiar scent or smell I couldn't identify, carried me to a childhood state of comfort and belonging.

Then, high above me, I heard sandhill cranes. I looked up

to see them in a ragged formation maybe half a mile high, flying hard with a northwest tailwind into the sun and crying their rattling, trumpet calls. The adults and their offspring, having spent the summer in the northern wetlands, might have been heading toward Yellow Springs on the way to wintering country in Florida and the Caribbean.

I walked a little further with Bella, and then I heard them again. This time, the cranes were in a perfect "V" and, it seemed to me, flying even higher and faster. They would certainly beat me to Ohio, I thought.

2010: Around the yard: the leave of pink-flowering spirea are yellow-ochre now, lamb's ear fresh and strong, young maple sapling still has its golden leaves, witch hazel leaves are rust brown and curled, its flowers gone, pale chartreuse sepals. Most forsythia gone, honeysuckle berries disappearing fast, oakleaf hydrangea leaves are still beautiful, maroon and deep forest green, flowering kale vigorous and still growing, pussy willow catkins halfway out like in late February. Most of the New England aster seeds are gone, and their leaves. False boneset is turning brown, the variegated viburnum yellow and dusky violet, orange winter berries against the stone wall, Osage leaves gradually thinning, still rust brown knotweed, some small white asters blooming by the old Russian sage.

2011: Crows after 8:00 a.m., cardinal calling in the back yard at 9:15. Rivers very high from days of rain, and the precipitation moves east, snarling Thanksgiving travel. About a third of the Osage and honeysuckle leaves left here at home, honeysuckle berries continue to fall all to the sidewalk, many still holding to their branches. On the way to Wisconsin this afternoon, just one hawk, two flocks of starlings seen.

2012: Liz Porter wrote at 2:10 p.m.: 'Two sandhill cranes flew over my house as I was hanging suet up in the maple tree! They gurgled/clucked/purred a little bit, and were high up going fast to the south and slightly east."

2013: Twenty-two crows came from the northeast in a tattered, broad pattern, the last bird flying late, calling to the others. Along Stafford Street, robins peeped in the honeysuckles, and starlings whistled in a bare maple.

2014: On the way out of town around noon: A huge flock of starlings and lots of crows feeding in the cutover soybean fields along Dayton-Yellow Springs Road. No other flocks seen between the village and Cincinnati.

2015: The Osage leaves came down throughout the day, an end to autumn in the yard.

2017: Sun and mild in the low 50s in Madison, Wisconsin. Jill and I walked along Lake Winga, a little ice on the water, no ducks.

2019: Crows before sunrise.

2020: Sun and chilly: Crows before sunrise. More than 200 geese on the pond, the full winter contingent.

2021: Drive to Madison, Wisconsin: one flock of turkey vultures seen circling, four small murmurations of starlings.

2022: Sandhill cranes sighted over southern Wisconsin as we drove toward Madison.

2023: Return from Madison, Wisconsin, under pale sun and mackerel sky the whole distance. On arrival home, I found all the white mulberry and the Osage leaves had fallen since I left on the 21st. The koi were shy in the pond, possibly from visits by the heron during my absence. But the net seems to have held, is still full of leaves.

Spirits among us have departed—friends, relatives, neighbors: we can't find them. If we search and call, the sky merely waits. Then some day here come the cranes planing in from cloud or mist—sharp, lonely spears, awkwardly graceful. They reach for

*the land; they stalk the ploughed fields, not letting us near, not
quite our own, not quite the world's.*

*People go by and pull over to watch. They peer and point and
wonder. It is because these travelers, these far wanderers, plane
down and yearn in a reaching flight. They extend our
life, piercing through space to reappear quietly, undeniably,
where we are.*

"Watching Sandhill Cranes" by William Stafford

Rain and wind gust.... The landscape was transformed. Only a touch of color remained here and there, the hills were austere and dark. Autumn was blown away like a shroud of dust, the earth was uncovered to the sky.

Harlan Hubbard

Sunrise/set: 7:30/5:13
Day's Length: 9 hours 43 minutes
Average High/Low: 47/31
Average Temperature: 39
Record High: 68 – 1931
Record Low: 3 – 1950

The Daily Weather

Today is cooler than the 23rd most years, with the arrival of the month's fifth major cold wave. Lows drop below freezing three nights out of four. Thirty-five percent of the afternoons reach above 50 degrees (rarely 60 degrees), 35 percent make the 40s, thirty percent are in the 30s. Chances of rain diminish to only 25 percent, but flurries come once every two decades. There is a 50/50 chance of mostly overcast conditions.

The Natural Calendar

Wild onions and the garden garlic grow a bit when the weather is mild. Fresh motherwort foliage is still strong. The grass along the freeways has turned pale, but winter wheat sometimes lengthens an inch or so, creating wide patches of green in the otherwise dormant landscape. The Christmas tree harvest has begun in Great Lakes region, trees filling the city nurseries. Throughout the Lower Midwest, farmers haul manure, and some fall tillage is still taking place on dry afternoons. Tobacco stripping continues in Kentucky and Tennessee.

1984: Silver maple leaves have finally all withered from the cold.

1985: Geese fly over honking at 8:24 a.m., more in the afternoon.

1986: Cardinal singing at 7:10 a.m.

1993: In Chicago yesterday, most of the honeysuckle leaves were gone. They are holding at maybe a fourth here. Forsythia leaves are coming down quickly in front of the house. Caraway in full bloom in the new fern bed. A giant dandelion found open beyond the butterfly preserve. A pileated woodpecker heard throughout my walk along the river, and sporadic robins, chickadees, cardinals.

1994: Walking upstream toward the covered bridge about four this afternoon: the sun had gone below the ridge behind me, and the valley was shaded except for the far bend of the river a few hundred yards ahead. The sun was shining there, and the white sycamores framed its brightness, making a kind of golden portal, an arch of light, inviting and warm. When I reached the river bend and walked out of the cold shade into the sun, I stood facing the bright west. I was part of the doorway, gold and warm like the ground and the trees. The November woods seemed complete to me then, the bare branches sufficient, glowing, welcoming, no longer less than summer green.

1997: Driving into Dayton today, I saw starlings flocking all along the highway. Snow last night, the second covering of a half an inch.

2001: Wisconsin: Willows done here, patches of hardy staghorns and Johnson grass. Hard south wind and hard rain. Below Chicago, visibility low, racing *stratus fractus*, then a great slice of blue, maybe the center of the low, then into lower stratus. Toward Bloomington, Illinois, into the sun and southwest wind. Above the stratus come cumulus, small shattered patches of clear sky. In the deeper openings: wispy, gossamer cirrus, then layers of fractus and cumulus, stratus so low I felt I was among them. I was riding in a window of rapidly closing from the west on my right, the dark gray circling around in front of me, closing. Near LaSalle, I approached another break in the clouds, could see deep blue then turquoise. A flock of blackbirds on my right, shaggy grasses leaning in the wind, geese here and there feeding. Leaves appeared on the trees south of Bloomington: honeysuckles and willows. Then, east of Indianapolis, I drove into the edge of the cyclone, dull gray and light rain all the way into Ohio.

2004: As the Thanksgiving cold front approaches, my barometer has dropped to 29.18, the lowest I've ever seen it. The temperature is 61, the wind rising, cold 40s just a few miles to the north.

2007: Returning from Wisconsin, I found the white mulberry tree had dropped all its leaves, probably after the hard freeze on the 22nd, 23rd or maybe even this morning. The Osage by the shed was about half down, still falling. Seven large hawks counted on the way home, but only a couple small flocks of starlings.

2009: Starlings whistling in the distance this morning. Privets and forsythia about half down, following the honeysuckles, which are dropping quickly. Osage leaves in back are holding well, as is the American beech in the park. The season of tufted small white asters has begun.

2010: A quiet morning, crows at 7:15, pink and gold altostratus clouds against the baby-blue sky, a few robins peeping when I walked Bella along Stafford Street. Most of the beech and pear leaves came down today. Heavy rain through the afternoon this Wednesday before Thanksgiving. Storms and snow in the Plains and Midwest.

2011: Madison, Wisconsin: The landscape here shows few differences with that of Yellow Springs, the autumn gentle in both places, the leaves falling at close intervals.

2012: In Madison, Tat's witch hazel still holds its flowers, but they are crinkled from the cold. In her back yard, a small, migrating flock of fox sparrows fed through the afternoon.

2013: The first morning in the teens: Osage fruit has started to turn murky gray-brown, thanks to the frost. Crows at 7:15 a.m. Clear sunrise, pink, golden streaks of clouds. Robins peeping behind the houses along Stafford Street. No sparrow or starling calls, but one song sparrow seen foraging in the dooryard leaves. The male cardinal is still attacking the reflective glass of my camper parked on the street.

2014: Hard wind, gusts rattling the tin roof, some brief downpours of rain, throughout the day as the November 24th cold front moved in. Noisy geese passed over the house several times in the morning and afternoon. When Bella and I were walking at Ellis Pond in the late afternoon, flocks of geese were restless, flying in a large circle around the park, honking all the while.

2015: Sparrows noticed on the front porch, seeming to feed on whatever is between the broken bricks. They have done that for many years, but I have never related it to the season.

2017: Madison, Wisconsin, sun, breezy and mild: Ginkgo fruits on the ground, mixed with leaves, on the way to the arboretum.

2019: Several hundred geese on the pond this afternoon, all of them abandoning their usual pasture in this mild and sunny spell before next week's gloom.

2020: Geese on the pond like last year. Walk with Jill at the state park: honeysuckle bushes, half shed, glowing a pale gray-green in the late afternoon, ghostly remnants of the year.

The language of cranes
we once were told
is the wind. The wind
is their method,
their current, the translated story
of life they write across the sky.

Linda Hogan

The last red leaf is whirl'd away,
The rooks are blown about the skies.

Alfred Lord Tennyson

Sunrise/set: 7:31/5:13
Day's Length: 9 hours 42 minutes
Average High/Low: 46/31
Average Temperature: 38
Record High: 71 – 1908
Record Low: 3 – 1950

The Daily Weather

Temperatures in the 60s return to Yellow Springs 15 percent of the time, make it into the 50s forty percent of the time, into the 40s twenty percent, into the 30s twenty percent, and into the 20s five percent of the time. The sun shines at least a little six to seven years in ten, and rain falls four to five days in ten. This is the date for the latest recorded frost in central Ohio.

The Natural Calendar

Even though this week is often one of the darkest and wettest of the Late Fall, milder autumns offer recollections as well as promises of spring.

Some years, garlic mustard has grown four or five inches tall, its leaves wide and bright. Chickweed has come back along the paths, and cress has revived in the pools and streams. Skunk cabbage has pushed up all over the swamp, some plants even opening a little. The low sun sets the new plants glowing like they glow in April.

Fed by honeysuckle berries and crab apples, robins linger in town and in the woods. Starlings cluck and whistle at sunrise, and cardinals and pileated woodpeckers and bobwhites sing off and on throughout the day.

1979: All the Osage leaves are finally down along King Street. All the forsythia, mock orange and honeysuckle are gone, too.

1980: Forsythia leaves all down.

1982: Chard and parsley finally hurt by frost. Comfrey prostrate, burned.

1984: South Glen: No skunk cabbage found so far. Mint, cress, dock, ragwort, garlic mustard, moneywort, sedum, ground ivy growing along the water. Hazy skies, temperatures in the 50s, it could be a day in March. A few oak leaves hang on, Norway maples hold some foliage. As I went toward High Prairie, I saw a deer running along the stream below, an arrow in its shoulder.

1986: Opossums still active at night, still being run over on Grinnell Road. Chubs bite, but no carp. The mild days are becoming more rare, skies darker.

1988: A cardinal sings at 11:56 a.m., then cardinals keep calling all day at home and in the woods, highs coming into the 60s, crickets chirping along the river, moths and flies common in the preserve.

1990: Purple deadnettle was blooming along the south wall, and a dandelion was open in the middle of the side lawn. A cardinal sang around 3:00.

1992: Cardinal singing at 7:28 a.m., gray morning, light rain, 42 degrees. Pear foliage continues to deteriorate slowly, now down to maybe a third.

1994: Starlings in the downtown trees this afternoon, the pears keeping most of their leaves in this warm and sunny autumn.

1999: Bradford pears are down to maybe half, yellowish-maroon in color. Starlings flocking in a tree on Davis and High Streets this afternoon. Osage leaves in the back yard hang on at maybe ten percent, all a heavy, vulnerable gold. One sweet gum tree a few blocks away has quite a few of its red leaves left.

2001: In Columbus, my white oaks are almost completely gone, and the small black grapes have fallen (or been eaten) from around my window. Along the freeway, honeysuckle leaves are more than half shed. At Washington Court House, the pear trees are at least two-thirds down.

2007: The downtown pear leaves are red and about half fallen. All of the front honeysuckle leaves are down, and the forsythia has been hurt by the hard freezes of the past two nights. In the south window of the bedroom, one Asian ladybeetle looks for a crevice in which to spend the winter. I saw one last week, too.

2008: Sudden increase in the falling of bittersweet hulls to the sidewalk.

2009: To Madison, Wisconsin in the rain, the landscape wet and fresh instead of frozen and hard the way I imagined it would be on this Thanksgiving drive. Before we left home, I noticed that the Osage tree had started to shed overnight.

2010: Steady rain through the night, the Osage tree in the back yard shedding hard, almost all the leaves gone.

2011: Returning from Wisconsin: One hawk, four large flocks of starlings and blackbirds, and two migrating flocks of gulls feeding in soybean fields. Honeysuckle leaves were absent until near Indianapolis. Dandelions blooming at an Illinois rest stop.

2013: Crows at 7:15 this clear, frosty morning.

2014: In the yard trees: a large flock of starlings, mixed with what appeared to be some robins and grackles, at about 9:00 this morning.

2016: I noticed that all the honeysuckle berries were down now, just as the leaf fall from the bushes intensified.

2017: Madison, Wisconsin to Yellow Springs: sun, steady wind, mild in the 50s throughout the Midwest. One large hawk, one large flock of what appeared to be cranes, one large murmuration of starlings, sightings of wildlife diminished compared to years past. Two insects killed on the car windshield during the trip. Throughout the countryside, oaks are keeping their leaves and creating a dense cover wherever those trees are dominant.

2018: John reported the first crane sighting of this year: "Saw (actually HEARD) them Sunday, Nov. 25th, at 11:20 a.m. As usual, my first response was, 'What the hell is that? A cuckoo?', and then the second time, I'm like, 'Oh -------, Sandhill Cranes!'

"I saw a pod of about twenty, probably an extended family group, at about a thousand feet, flying from west to east, just south of my property. Ran screaming to the house for Jane to come out. When I cam back outside, they were calling and tracking on the same path, but from east to west. Getting their bearings I guess. Earliest sighting for me. I'm guessing they were bugging out in advance of what The Weather Channel is calling Winter Storm Bruce coming at us through the Plains."

Emily emailed a little later: "I was pleased and overjoyed to hear a flock of 20 bugling big birds, way high in the sky. As I was breathing and relaxing in my sit spot, there they were, kettling in the north, making their way over YS and toward the SW. By the flash of white and black on the wings, I guessed that maybe they were Tundra Swans."

2019: Lil's maple, my Osage and Rachel's silver maple are scraggly. The oaks are brown and dull. Before sunrise: robins peeping, a cardinal call far off.

2022: Mild Thanksgiving weather throughout the Midwest, starlings eating crabapples at the motel.

Stood amazed at the quiet, the bright sun, the spring-like light. The sharp outline of the pasture. Knolls, the brightness of bare trees in the hopeful sun.

Thomas Merton, November 25, 1967

November 26th
The 330th Day of the Year

When woods are bare and birds are flown,
And frosts and shortening days portend
The aged year is near his end....

William Cullen Bryant

Sunrise/set: 7:32/5:12
Day's Length: 9 hours 40 minutes
Average High/Low: 46/30
Average Temperature: 38
Record High: 70 – 1990
Record Low: 8 – 1930

The Daily Weather

When the final weather system of the month approaches Ohio, November 26th is one of the windiest and warmest days in late November. Temperatures reach 70 five percent of the time, the 60s thirty percent, and the 50s twenty percent. Cool 40s are recorded 25 percent of the afternoons; 30s come on 20 percent. Clouds keep out the sun one day in two; rain falls four days in a decade. Frost strikes only 25 percent of the years, the last time in the year when the incidence of freezing temperatures is so low.

The Natural Calendar

Sandhill Crane Migrating Season begins in portions of the Lower Midwest as November fades. Crow Gathering Season approaches as thousands of crows congregate to spend the winter, their advent announced by the conclusion of Witch Hazel Flowering Season, by Beech Tree Shedding Season, New England Aster Foliage Yellowing Season, the Season of Orange Euonymus Berries (their white outer shells falling away in the cold), Christmas Tree Harvest Season and the final cabbage butterfly of Cabbage Butterfly Season. Throughout the Lower Midwest, the severity of late autumn cold dictates the progress of the final losses of foliage and the dropping of fruits, and appears to influence the schedule of cranes, gulls, crows and starlings.

1979: Forsythia and pie cherry leaves are down.

1982: No cabbage worms found on the kale. The cabbage butterflies have completed their cycles.

1985: Waterleaf growing in the yard. Becky's white birch has only a few leaves left.

1986: All across the county, the tree lines (except where oaks predominate) are totally black, ready for December. Downtown, the pears are losing their leaves, two of them almost bare. Roadside grass is mostly yellow or tan now.

1988: All of the last Osage leaves fell today.

1992: To northern Illinois, pear trees throughout are yellow, hold at maybe half their leaves.

1994: The final flowers shrivel on the witch hazel. Last year in the cold, they held through December. In this year's warmth, their peak was over a couple of weeks ago. One mum, the white in the south garden, is still in bloom, a few pink yarrow are still fresh along the north fence, a few rose buds still look promising beside them.

2001: Returning from a Thanksgiving reunion in Wisconsin, I drove into the eye of a low-pressure system that was moving from west to east. Barometric lows appear like dips or troughs on a graph, and when you ride the low, you travel inside the bottom of its hollow core and can watch it spin heavily around you.

This late morning, I came south through a wall of rain out into the windswept opening of sky and clouds. Behind me and on my right and left, the horizon was dark. My road went straight into the white horizon toward a nucleus of blue that slowly dissolved to gossamer cirrus broken by intrusions of *stratus fractus*, jagged and torn by the wind and so low I felt I was flying through them.

The eyelid of the storm opened and shut for hours.

Sometimes the sun appeared, and I moved into a swell of light, and the plowed prairie around me glowed in patches, then quieted again as my position changed. I passed into new breaches and between waves, long banks of gray and sun, now cirrus and altostratus, then tufted, broken, piled cumulus, some bright, some black, shapes from childhood, shaggy angels, anvils, whales, rabbits, snowmen, cottony jumbles.

The grass beside me leaned and quivered. Whitecaps rose on the farm ponds. The rain pools on the roadsides rippled in the hard southeast wind. A flock of crows came over, later blackbirds. Gulls in one field, geese in another, waited for the storm to subside.

When I turned east to Indianapolis, I reached the leading side of the front, the wind shifted to the southwest, the windows of light closed, and the sky turned flat and dull. The rain started. Through the day, I had cut down from the northern rim of the great spinning low into its heart, and then to its foremost edge. Before it could engulf me again, I pierced its side and emerged ahead of it as the afternoon ended. Here in Yellow Springs when I went to bed, the front caught up with me, and as I went to sleep, I imagined the moon shining in its eye.

2004: Robins still common, peeping in the honeysuckles.

2007: I noticed that the beech on Dayton Street had lost all its leaves – probably when we were gone and at the same time the white mulberry came down, around the 23rd or 24th.

2010: The final Osage leaves trickled down throughout the day, only a handful left at sundown. In front of the shed, I found the first Osage fruit shredded by the squirrels. All the mums are finally gone.

2011: Robins peeping after dawn. I raked Osage leaves this afternoon, only a few left. Planted a handful of hyacinths in the back between the redbud trees. Soft and windy day, with a high in the low 60s. Bob Parker stopped me this morning, said he'd been finding "all kinds of mushrooms" growing - more than any year he could remember. And a friend of his had a white iris blooming two weeks ago. Bob Barcus called at 4:30, said he had a stump full of what he thought were shitake mushrooms. I told him to call Bob Parker for a positive ID.

2013: At the college parking lot, the bodies of worms driven out by the last hard rains before the cold.

2012: Driving from Madison to Yellow Springs: no murmurations of starlings this trip, but many small flocks of geese seen, and four white-breasted hawks.

2014: Driving from Yellow Springs to Madison: Four murmurations of starlings (one very large), one substantial murder of crows, and two large hawks. All the pear and white oak leaves along the way were aged dark brown from the cold.

2016: Madison to Yellow Springs: Relatively mild temperatures throughout the Midwest today. A hard southwest headwind to central Illinois, then mostly at our back east to home. As we dropped down from Bloomington towards Indianapolis, more color appeared in the tree lines: oaks, pears and Norway maples. At the last rest stop before Indianapolis, crab apples had recently fallen onto the sidewalk, perhaps the work of a flock of starlings, and leaves were falling heavily from a Norway maple. I found three dandelion flowers huddled in the cropped grass when we stopped to get gas.

2017: I woke up to a robin by the koi pond fountain. Crows were loud and insistent. On the other side of Dayton Street, starlings and blackbirds chattering.

2020: My forsythia bushes still close me off from the street, so in my room I can hold on to the old year from behind my window. Advent is three days away. I wonder about putting up an Advent Wreath again, wonder about winter, about ordering seeds. Do I really want a garden again? A psychological space between the year's end and the next beginning, a tiredness settling over me. Maybe I'm ready for winter, maybe looking ahead to spring is the wrong thing to do.

2021: Graphs of barometric pressure reveal many of the topographic patterns of the season. This year's Middle Fall dissolved into the rains and the warmth of October's last days. Leaf color peaked at the same time (the latest in decades), and then the first great barometric high of Late Fall arrived to dominate the first ten days of November.

Drawn by the tidal power of the new moon, the barometric pressure reached 30.40 inches, the tallest crest in months, bringing five days of frosty mornings and the first killing freeze on November 3. This massive weather system became a lazy slope by the 8th, and its soft decline produced temperatures in the 60s and 70s until the barometric pressure tumbled into an atmospheric trough, accompanied by hard rain and then rose abruptly to a snow-capped peak on the 13th.

Then warmth returned as the pressure fell in advance of lunar perigee and full moon and the eclipse of the 20th, and then the barometric graph revealed another vast rise, the greatest since last winter, 30.55 inches, followed quickly by a precipice that fell off into the gentle Thanksgiving thaw and then sharply rose again with the cold snap of the 26th.

And as that new mountain pushed up out of the air, the first sandhill cranes came migrating over Yellow Springs, riding the ebbing of the moon and the canyons of wind that surged and collapsed into the waves of oncoming Early Winter.

(Today at 3:21 p.m., Bob called: "I think I just heard and saw about 26 sandhill cranes go over. Well, I guess they were sandhill cranes; they had a kind of a soft turkey-like gobbling sound, and they were going directly from north to south over our place.")

2022: Returning from Wisconsin, we were covered by a great murder of crows in downtown Urbana, Illinois at dusk.

I'm starting to see more clearly the interpretation I put on physical events like the weather. There is physical weather – sun, rain, wind – that just is, and my emotional response – pleasure, peace, anger, anxiety – that I associate with the weather. If I can tease these aspects apart, and experience weather as weather and emotional response as emotional response, my days might be less dramatic and draining.

Robert Kull

November 27th
The 331st Day of the Year

At the eleventh hour, late in the year, we have visions of the life we might have lived.

Henry David Thoreau

Sunrise/set: 7:34/5:11
Day's Length: 9 hours 37 minutes
Average High/Low: 45/30
Average Temperature: 38
Record High: 74 – 1990
Record Low: 0 – 1930

The Daily Weather

This is the rainiest day in my record for the entire year in Yellow Springs, with precipitation (but almost never snow) noted 70 percent of the time. Highs in the 70s occur five to ten percent of the years, 60s twenty percent, 50s thirty percent, 40s thirty-five percent, 30s five to ten percent. Clouds dominate the sky, allowing sun to come through just four days out of ten. Morning lows dip under 32 degrees four days in ten, as well.

The Natural Calendar

From this point, growth, even among the winter plants like purple deadnettle and henbit, dock, dandelions, is almost imperceptible in average years, and the cold does away with all their November progress.

The beeches and the pears are often gone, and the silver maples and the oaks thin out. Forsythia and spirea turn deep red and yellow from the frost. Tangled bittersweet, foliage gone, is wide open along the fencerows. Wisteria leaves fall with the bittersweet. Bright pink coralberries shine through the undergrowth. Seed tufts of virgin's bower complement tufts of milkweed, thimble plants and cattails. Winterberry berries are bright orange, their hulls swelling.

1984: Most Osage and mock orange leaves suddenly gone.

1985: Most Osage hold, many mock orange, forsythia still strong, affected by the lack of frost. A third of the poplars have kept their leaves.

1988: Paperwhites, started on the 22nd at two inches, are up to five inches now.

1990: Almost all the downtown pear leaves have fallen in piles along the sidewalks. Only the last willows and Osage hold. But the grass is beginning to grow after a long warm spell in the 60s and 70s. Yesterday and today the cardinals were singing more, overcome by this early thaw.

1993: All the rest of the Osage leaves fell this week. Fresh chickweed, which sprouted at the end of the summer, is blooming here and there in the yard and in the woods.

1997: A cardinal sang at 7:05 this morning, accompanied by a rooster to the west. In the pond, the fish came up to feed today, swam at the top for a while; Emmett even took a leap out of the water - then settled back to the bottom with the others. Two moths came to the front window last night, even though the temperature was in the 40s. This morning, I found one of them in an old spider web. As I slowly removed the web from around it, the moth flew away.

1999: The New England aster foliage turned yellow in early November; now its leaves are falling. The gooseneck plant turns chocolate brown.

2000: All but one of the sweet gum trees are bare now. Japanese maple down to just a few leaves. Burning bush finally complete.

2004: A few hours fishing for catfish at Caesar Creek this afternoon with John. The barometer was dropping, the wind hard from the south, shifting to the east. The sun was out for a little while, then was covered by altocumulus clouds. The temperature remained steady at about 50 degrees, and we were chilled after only an hour on shore. No bites, but a few boats were out on the water near the dam. A flock of gulls circled back and forth along the channel, the only birds seen.

2006: After almost a week of mild, sunny weather in the 50s and 60s, the koi rose to be fed this morning. Walking in the alley with Bella, I listened to starlings and robins the whole way. Dandelions were still flowering at Moya's; the purple crocus was still open at the north end of the house.

2009: Madison, Wisconsin: the fall has been mild here, deadnettle in full bloom, as in Yellow Springs. Willows are gold and thinning. Tat's witch hazel flowers are shriveled. Casey left a message on the answering machine today: Sandhill cranes at 2:50 this afternoon, maybe 40 in all circling round and round in big, long, lazy circles.

2012: Back from Madison to find the pear leaves all down, and at Ellis Pond the willow leaves are finally gone, and the sawtooth oak is down to only about half its foliage. No more beach leaves on the Dayton Street tree, almost all the honeysuckle bushes bare. The Osage remnant from October is shriveled but holding fast. The setting sun at Ellis Pond was yellow and blue-gray this afternoon through the altostratus. Lori Deal reported seeing sandhill cranes today at her home near John Bryan Park.

2013: On the road to Wisconsin: I saw five sandhill cranes flying in a diamond formation southeast over I-70 near Huber Heights at 8:15 this morning, a great murmuration of starlings a few miles later. A large murder of crows seen in Illinois. Snow and sun throughout the trip, all leaves gone. And Mary White left a phone message saying she had seen twenty sandhills heading south as she "ran around the block" about 2:30 in the afternoon. Then her e-mail: "Soon after that – about 3:00 - I saw about 60 more. Both groups seemed to be taking advantage of the tailwind – a stiff wind from the north that afternoon. But they are right on schedule! Always amazes me."

2016: Home from Madison, mild and bright sun: While we were gone, all the white mulberry leaves, all the wisteria leaves, all the bittersweet leaves, and most of the pink quince leaves, and the leaves from Lil's maple (except the shriveled ones) and Jeanie's birch came down, were most likely taken by the rain that travelled with the cold front of the 23rd.

2017: Wisteria leaves and many Osage leaves still hold, dull brown and curled. Zelcova, oak and pear foliage is still quite full. Pokeweed stalks are a dusky ochre, knotweed stalks rusty red.

2018: Yesterday, the first snow-bearing front of winter came through, maybe an inch or so on the ground, barometer rising, temps in the 20s. I saw the first junco of the season in the circle garden. And Casey called at 10:15 this morning from Polecat Road, just outside of the village, said that he had heard sandhills yodeling above the clouds. He called back ten minutes later to say he saw them circling over Ellis Pond (which is down Polecat Road. Then Betty Ross called to say she had seen 27 sandhill cranes when she was on the bike trail near the Glen Helen building. "Nicest line of cranes I've ever seen," she said.

2020: Robins all around as I walked outside this gentle, gray morning. The alley was bare and damp, fallen leaves raked to the sides or scattered away into yards, the world around me motionless, it seemed, in the aftermath of Thanksgiving, in the aftermath of the final drop of the late foliage. Koi still feeding eagerly, in spite of water temperatures in the 50s. On the way to the quarry in this mild afternoon, a long flock of starlings seen flying from the west.

2021: Return drive from Madison, Wisconsin: light rain all the way, four small flocks of starlings seen, occasional crows and "V"s of geese. At home, I found the white mulberry leaves and most of the Osage leaves had come down in the five days we were gone. Some zelcovas and beech leaves hold, but leaf drop is basically over.

2022: Near Enon, huge murmuration of starlings flew over as we were returning from a trip to Wisconsin. And a message from Erin, Alisha and Ellis when we arrived home: "Very large starling murmuration today 11/27 on William & Mary Ct. It was beautiful to watch." They included a video that lasted and lasted, thousands of birds swooping and calling, landing and taking off.

2023: First flurries in town. From Madison, Wisconsin, Tat sends a photo of a giant snowman made from their perfect snowfall.

Although it rarely occupies our full attention, the weather is always evident at the periphery of that attention, an ever-present reminder that the reality we inhabit is ultimately beyond our human control.

David Abram

November 28th
The 332nd Day of the Year

When all the snowy hill
And the bare woods are still,
When snipes are silent in the frozen bogs,
And all the garden garth is whelmed in mire,
Lo, by the hearth, the laughter of the logs,
More fair than roses, lo, the flowers of fire!

R. L. Stevenson

Sunrise/set: 7:34/5:11
Day's Length: 9 hours 37 minutes
Average High/Low: 45/30
Average Temperature: 37
Record High: 68 – 1909
Record Low: 4 – 1887

The Daily Weather

The sixth cold wave of the month generally reaches the Ohio Valley by this date, and the next two days are often the coldest of the month. Forty-five percent of the highs are only in the 30s, and 30 percent are in the 40s. Afternoons warm to the 50s on 15 percent of the afternoons, reach the 60s ten percent. Snow falls 20 percent of the years; rain occurs 25 percent. And the sun shines less frequently on this day than on any other day in the entire year in southwest Ohio: less than 30 percent of the time.

The Natural Calendar

Advent, the Christian vigil season for Christmas, begins at the end of November or the first days of December, and it parallels a period of radical change in local weather.

On December 2nd, close to Advent's first Sunday, the sun reaches its earliest setting of the year in Yellow Springs and continues to set at the same time for twelve days. Then on the 14th of the month, just before Advent's third Sunday (the *Gaudete* or rejoicing Sunday), sunset begins to occur a minute later every two or three days.

This small advance, however, is offset by the sun rising later in the morning. And the point-counterpoint of time lost and gained creates a weeklong standoff around winter solstice during which the day's length remains its shortest of the year in this location, nine hours and twenty minutes.

Christmas day, the fulfillment of Advent, marks the end of these darkest days, and on the feast of St. Stephen, December 26th, daylight begins to increase for the first time since the end of June.

Sunrise, however, keeps taking place slightly later up until New Year's Eve. Finally, within the octave of Epiphany, the last of the major Christmas celebrations, mornings finally lengthen. The reversal of the sun's course and the 40-day vigil for its turn toward summer are complete.

By ten o'clock at night in late November, the winter stars have moved deep into the sky. The Pleiades are almost overhead, leading on the Hyades, Taurus, and Aldebaran. Orion towers in the southeast, followed by Sirius and Procyon. Castor and Pollux, the rulers of January, stand above Orion's hounds. Summer's Dolphin is pursuing Altair into the west. October's Fomalhaut sinks into the southwest, directly below the Great Square. August's Vega is setting. Cygnus, the swan of the Northern Cross, and the lanky gauge of autumn's progress, is disappearing south. Pegasus and Andromeda fall away behind it.

Zeitgeber Wreathing

The ancient season of Advent parallels the beginning of the natural year throughout the Northern Hemisphere. Many people follow this period with a wreath of five candles, four to mark each Sunday before Christmas and a fifth to light at the celebration of the birth of Christ.

One complement to this tradition is to increase the number of candles to twelve, each one suggesting a different step in the progress of the year toward Early Spring. Lighting a different candle at dinner each week between now and the second week of February not only brightens the evenings but offers a framework for creating time with zeitgebers (events in nature) that define it.

Week 1
Beech and pear leaves fall.
Week 2
Sandhill cranes fly over the Ohio Valley as Early Winter begins.
Week 3
The sun begins to set later in the day (but the sun continues to rise later in the morning).
Week 4
Winter Solstice occurs during the shortest days of the year, and the sun enters Capricorn.
Week 5
The day begins to lengthen.
Week 6
Deep Winter, the coldes time of year, arrives.
Week 7
Titmice initiate their mating songs.
Week 8
Giant pileated woodpeckers mate as the sun comes into Aquarius.
Week 9
The January Thaw arrives with Late Winter, and average temperatures start to rise.
Week 10
Cardinals and doves sing before dawn.
Week 11
Bluebirds migrate to the Lower Midwest.
Week 12
The sun enters Pisces, and Early Spring comes to the United States, accompanied by red-winged blackbirds, flowing maple sap and flowering snowdrops.

Daybook

1983: Pear leaves are rich brown along Xenia Avenue. Most forsythia foliage is gone.

1990: No geese heard in four or five days. Maybe their fall restlessness is over now. Osage leaves coming down in clumps.

1992: One periwinkle seen blooming in front of Tat's house in Chicago. Long flock of blackbirds seen in central Indiana, a huge "V" of geese as I approached Indianapolis.

1993: First striped-breasted sparrow of the season seen at the bird feeder today.

1997: The blackened lilac leaves have finally come down. The forsythia hedge is almost empty. Privets are bare, their blue berries standing out. Crows came through the neighborhood at 7:30 sharp this morning.

2000: Pear trees in Springfield darkening and starting to lose their leaves. Beech and English oak down to maybe just ten percent. Last sweet gum finally breaking down. At school, one ladybug and one fly on the staircase windows. Two dandelions open in the grass in spite of the gray and cold and wind.

2002: Five large hawks counted on the way to Wisconsin. The roadside grass throughout the trip was bright green. In the Madison arboretum, geese flew back and forth during our walk.

2004: All the rest of the beech leaves collapsed this weekend, and the downtown pears have lost more than half of their foliage (their color is still red – not the brown of twenty years ago). Jerry and Lee's sweet gum is down to just a handful of leaves. The Zelcovas that line the south part of Xenia Avenue are shedding in tandem with the pears and beeches.

2005: The downtown pear trees have lost about half their foliage, their color mostly green. Only a few fragments remain on other trees (beeches, mock orange, Osage and sweet gums all down). It was warm and windy today. I planted ten late tulips in the east garden. The koi began to move around and feed as the rain arrived late in the afternoon.

  This evening, a woman called from Grinnell Circle, said that she had seen about thirty sandhill cranes flying over the South Glen heading south along the river. It was around noon, and she was walking the Sontag's dog that she was caring for over the holiday.

"I know that sound," she said. "I heard it in South Dakota."

They were flying "higher than buzzards," and she went to get her binoculars; by the time she returned they were almost out of sight. "You know them when you hear them," she said, but she returned to the house, listened to her CD of bird calls to double-check her identification. And she wondered if other people had called in with the sighting. Even though she has taught birding, "It's always good to have another birder tell you you're right."

2007: Crisp morning, frost on the fallen leaves. I counted twenty starlings in Don's alley tree. Two crows came by about 7:30 a.m. All of the burning bush leaves have fallen in the past week, and the bittersweet leaves and orange hulls are on the sidewalk. The hostas are dissolving into the ground, and the brown stonecrop plants are falling over. Out in town, pansies and flowering kale have held on well. After walking Bella, I moved the two birdfeeders from the west corner of the back yard into the front garden. In the afternoon, I mowed the lawn, mulching the leaves that covered it. Seven firm amaryllis bulbs taken from the garden, their tops badly burned from the frost. I planted them and brought them indoors to see how they would do. A large starling flock along the way to Enon late in the afternoon.

2009: Returning from Madison, Wisconsin, full sun, the temperature in the 50s all the way home. In spite of today's history as the cloudiest day of the year – not a cloud in sight during the whole 500-mile trip. Half a dozen large hawks seen, but few flocks of birds. Fields rich brown, most harvest complete, the green along the highway like spring green, pear trees holding their many of their leaves from central Indiana east and south, willows keeping some pale green leaves – they were gold and getting bare in Wisconsin. Throughout the Midwest, the autumn has been mild, John telling me that Lanesboro in Minnesota has had the warmest November on record.

2010: Crows at 7:35, cardinal and tufted titmouse singing near sunrise. Almost all the pear leaves downtown have fallen now.

2011: Heavy rains throughout the area, worms driven up from the ground, sprawling across the sidewalk on High Street and Dayton Street.

2012: All of the last leaves of the backyard Osage came down overnight, lie in a withered, yellow-green quilt across the southwest corner of the property. Sunny and frosty today. Walked with Jeff at a small wetland park in Xenia, saw a large, white-breasted hawk, the land free of leaves, cattails coming apart. At Ellis Pond, the sawtooth oak is down to maybe just a third of its leaves. Tonight, Jill Downey called to report a sighting of sandhill cranes above John Bryan Park. Jill's was the third report of cranes so far this year.

2015: In Madison, Wisconsin, Tat's oakleaf hydrangeas keep their soft, red-purple-brown leaves.

2016: A pair of starlings burbling as I walked down Limestone Street from Jill's house this morning. No reports of cranes so far his autumn. Downtown pears are deep ochre and gold. The Dayton Street beech keeps about half its foliage. Along Xenia Avenue, many Zelcovas have kept their leaves, and many sweet gums hold at about a third. The red of burning bush shrubs still adds to the village landscape. Bittersweet berries stand out now, strung across the branches of the High Street redbuds, a sudden revelation because of the latest leafdrop.

2017: From the high ridge at John Bryan Park, the land is summer green from honeysuckles that keep their foliage. In town, the post office pears are more than half down, and the Zelcovas thin quickly. Robins and starlings create backdrop to the afternoon at home, one murmuration seen. One forsythia bush in full bloom on Park Place, and one forsythia flower on my hedge. Like most of the days this past week, sun and mild, nothing like the dark and cold rain of years ago on this date.

2019: Sedum seeds are dark now ready to scatter, their stalks weak and leaning, their leaves changing from pale green to ochre to mottled brown.

2020: Chris Walker reported seeing two Trumpeter Swans on Kiser Lake this past week.

2022: A note about this day in 2002: No large hawks seen for years on the trips to Madison, Wisconsin.

2023: First morning in the teens, ice on the far end of the koi pond. From northern Minnesota, John reports ice on his bay at Vermillion Lake.

So let us go on
though the sun be swinging east,
And the ponds be cold and black,
and the sweets of the year be doomed.

Mary Oliver, from "Lines written in the Days of Growing Darkness"

They will come again, the leaf and the flower, to arise
From squalor of rottenness into the old splendour,
And magical scents to a wondering memory bring;
The same glory, to shine upon different eyes.
Earth cares for her own ruins, naught for ours.
Nothing is certain, only the certain spring.

Laurence Binyon

Sunrise/set: 7:35/5:11
Day's Length: 9 hours 36 minutes
Average High/Low: 45/29
Average Temperature: 37
Record High: 70 – 1927
Record Low: - 2 – 1887

The Daily Weather

Today is a usually a chilly day, with a 70 percent chance of freezing morning temperatures. Precipitation comes four years in ten, half the time as rain, the other half as snow. Highs are in the 60s or 70s just five percent of the time, in the 50s ten percent, in the 40s forty-five percent, in the 30s thirty percent, the 20s ten percent. Skies are completely overcast 40 percent of the years. Low temperatures in southwestern Ohio can fall below zero between this date and March 20th.

The Natural Calendar
Counting absences
Days without red-winged blackbirds
Autumn Samadhi

The inventory of middle autumn at the end of October is rich in foliage and color, but the settling in of late autumn in November draws down the density and texture of the canopy and strips away almost all the floral barriers to winter. As spring overcomes February and March with an accumulation of new growth, fall spreads across the summer with an accumulation of loss.

One enumeration of late fall is the counting of what no longer holds, a counting of emptiness, cued only by memory and the more durable, woody scaffolding that binds the seasons:

Foliage of apple trees and crab apple trees, ginkgoes, sugar maples, trees of heaven, redbuds, black walnuts, catalpas, box elders, locusts, elms, birches, poplars, cottonwoods, peach trees, cherry trees, Osage, red oaks, white oaks, chinquapin oaks sycamores, red mulberries, sweet gums, silver maples, Japanese maples, white mulberry trees, beeches, magnolias, mock orange and silver olive shrubs, honeysuckles, Korean lilacs, quinces, privets, viburnums, burning bush, dogwoods, spireas, standard lilacs, down or collapsing –

Silent mornings: no more robins chattering, no cardinal song, no dove song, no red-winged blackbird song, no grackle song, no cicada song, no katydid song, no cricket song –

Hollow milkweed pods, bare raspberry canes, bare blackberry canes, the leaves of hostas and stonecrop melted, innumerable flowers absent, and harvest complete – no wheat, soybeans, corn, tomatoes, peas, beans, cucumbers, zucchini, lettuce.

Daybook

1982: The garden is ready for spring, the weeds all pulled, vines and stalks thrown on the compost, asparagus cut back, manure and shredded leaves dug under, pathways set, the earth smoothed over. The summer's garlic, planted in October, is half a foot tall. Spinach is sown for March. Worms have come to work the topsoil, sparrows clean the last seeds and the grass snakes are sleeping in the stone wall. Parsley and thyme are mulched deep with straw.

1988: Paperwhites are nine inches tall today: they started at two inches on the 22nd. The amaryllis, begun on the 13th, has grown 13 inches. Winter sundogs seen in the late afternoon sky.

1990: First mother-of-millions noticed flowering in the greenhouse.

1991: On the way from St. Louis home: long flocks of blackbirds near the Mississippi.

1992: House finches (four of them at the thistle seed this morning).

1993: First junco seen at the feeder today, and the first wren since early in the summer.

1995: Cardinal singing at 8:00 this morning, and again fifteen minutes later. At the triangle park, the tips of the spruce branches have more new needles now, quite a bit of progress since I first noticed growth in October. At the corner of Limestone and High Streets, bittersweet continues to fall to the sidewalk. Along Dayton Street, the yellow witch hazel flowers are shriveling.

2000: Thunder with flurries this morning, a flicker of spring or remnant of summer, just as the landscape settles down to December and January stasis.

2001: Pear leaves are red and gold downtown, thinned to maybe just a fourth of their summer number.

2004: Around the yard, some Osage and mock orange still hang on, but the lilacs are finally down. Parsley is still bright under the old apple tree, and lavender is still blooming in the garden over on the corner. I saw a few purple asters blooming around town yesterday. The soil thermometer near the pond says 43 degrees, its lowest reading of the fall.

2005: Robins still calling and flying around the Stafford Street alley before sunrise. One robin even gave a long singsong call a few days ago, maybe on the 25th.

2007: No robins seen or heard for almost a month. About fifty or more starlings in Don's trees this morning, the most I've seen there. Some of the pear trees downtown are bare, some about three-fourths fallen. Two orange woolly bear caterpillars found in the flowerpots outside yesterday; I put them in the hollow of the old apple tree stump. Paperwhites planted today.

2008: Madison to Yellow Springs: Five large hawks, three or four large flocks of waterfowl resting in ponds and small lakes, one large flock of crows in central Illinois, two small flocks of starlings. Landscape uniform throughout.

2009: First day home after returning from Madison. The Osage tree has shed much more, but still keeps maybe a fourth of its leaves. The coneflowers in the alley hold on, unfazed by the date. Starlings whistle in the Stafford Street trees. Jonatha, just back from Japan, said the ginkgoes there two weeks ago were golden but had not started to fall, about a week or so behind the ones in Yellow Springs.

2010: Crows at 7:30 this morning, half a dozen robins in the Danielsons' bare maple at 8:00.

2011: The first snow of the year late this afternoon, the ground white for a few hours before the wet grass soaked it up. More worms stranded from the earlier rain.

2012: Continued cool and sunny. Background whistling from starlings in the neighborhood. In the Stafford/Phillips Street alley, bittersweet hulls have fallen, orange berries decking the honeysuckle trellis.

2014: Returning to Yellow Springs from Wisconsin in bright sun, snow all across the landscape, I saw maybe five miles of waves of sandhill cranes flying fairly low across the Illinois fields about a hundred miles south of Madison. Later, two flocks of gulls far off on farm ponds. No large flocks of starlings, no hawks seen.

2015: Returning from Wisconsin: only two hawks seen, no starlings, no gulls, no cranes.

2016: Light breeze and mild in the low 60s: Lil's and Peggy's burning bush foliage collapsed during the night rain. Robin peeping in the yard around noon. The seeds from small white asters disappear. The yellow ochre leaves of the New England asters have started to fall. This afternoon, I stacked some wood and worked in the garden taking out aster stalks.

2017: Another day of sun and mild temperatures. The post office pears and Zelcovas are about down, but Peggy's and many others are still gold and bright. Lil's maple has just a few leaves left, and the Dayton Street beech is down to about a fourth.

2019: All around the yard, the honeysuckle leaves have fallen. John Blakelock reports a small flock of meadow larks flying south, seeming to play and chase each other as they travelled.

2020: Barometer dropping in advance of tomorrow's full moon storm, sun, mackerel sky, cirrus and mild 50s. At the Covered Bridge, four turkey vultures circling so high. In the muck near the stream, slim skunk cabbage has appeared, six inches at the tallest. Throughout the woods, chickweed spreading. Beyond the woods, the pasture is bright green in today's sun. The river is late-November high, deeper than I've seen it this fall. In the back yard, the Osage tree has lost most of its leaves, only a couple of branches holding yellow green. Past the graveyard, four dandelions blooming by the gravel path.

2021: Robins are still here. I heard them peeping in the honeysuckles today. Jill reports four small murmurations of starlings on her drive from the city.

2023: Osage fruits have started to yellow. Honeysuckles are losing more foliage, leaves paler, yellower.

Like absences and spaces between sounds, unconnected events and events out of apparent context create an emptiness that is both expectant and complete.

Leon Quel

November 30th
The 334th Day of the Year

Comes with evening now
Out of the afterglow
the west wind growing:
Over the hill and the red hawthorn
over the stubbled field and the brown shocked corn,
from Venus dreaming in the smoldering sky
the wind comes mourning.

August Derleth

Sunrise/set: 7:36/5:11
Day's Length: 9 hours 35 minutes
Average High/Low: 44/29
Average Temperature: 37
Record High: 69 – 1934
Record Low: - 2 – 1958

The Daily Weather
Temperatures reach the 60s on ten percent of the days, climb to the 50s fifteen percent, to the 40s forty percent, to the 30s thirty percent, to the 20s five percent. The sun shines half the time, and rain comes 15 percent of the days, snow another 15 percent. Two nights out three, lows drop below freezing.

The Natural Calendar
The gooseneck loosestrife turns chocolate brown. Most all the seeds are gone from milkweed pods; just a few wisps of down cling to their shells. Fragile pokeweed stems have exploded in the frost. Yellow witch hazel flowers shrivel. Privets are bare, their blue berries revealed. Euonymus fruits lose their white outer pods more quickly, orange cores unveiled by the cold. The last roses have usually been frozen by nights in the teens.

Daybook
1982: Grinnell Mill: Chickweed and dandelions flowering. Spring foliage found up river: mint, hemlock, henbit, clover, thistle,

yarrow, purple deadnettle, sweet rocket, garlic mustard, leafcup, sedum, dock, parsnip, moneywort, waterleaf, avens.

1984: Beech leaves hang on this year, maybe a third. Mums killed by hard freeze, also the broccoli, petunias, alyssum. A few forsythia flowers hold. All Osage and mock orange done. Sweet gum trees at the art institute have a just few leaves left.

1985: Birch leaves gone.

1986: Forsythia noticed gone, all honeysuckle too.

1989: Cardinal sings once at 8:08 a.m., the morning sunny, garden covered with frost. The pear leaves have all fallen downtown, the Christmas lights can shine through. Forsythia, honeysuckle, mock orange, Osage have all come down in the last ten days. In the greenhouse, two new geraniums have bloomed; tomatoes are full size, still green. October zinnias wilting, mums and impatiens a little stalky. Most coleus killed by mealy bugs. Lettuce under lights, brought in from the garden October 15th, has remained strong. The violet hibiscus blossoms every few days.

1992: Sparrow hawk seen on the telephone wires along Wilberforce-Clifton, first of the season.

1997: After three days of temperatures in the 60s, the first front of December approaches tonight. Pears thinning downtown.

1998: A November of grace - clear skies and warm temperatures. All of the light lately has been the special light that Derleth talks about "during that recessive period of the year."

1999: All but a few dozen lilac leaves have come down now. All but two of the poplars fell in this last cold wave, the last of the Osage too, and the beech has just a few patches of lower leaves. With temperatures in the teens tonight, the pears are next.

2000: Two ladybugs in the stairwell window at school. Along the bike path, three-fourths of the honeysuckle leaves are down.

2001: Three turkey vultures seen on the way back from Fairborn this morning. They were riding on the hard west wind.

2004: All these notes, for what? Sometimes I think I am no more linear than the moon and stars around me. Even though it seems my life progresses in a line from start to finish, actually it rises and falls and rises and falls again and again along some mysterious ecliptic on a beach with leaf and berry tides.

2005: A brisk, raw day: The starlings were gone from their tree this morning, and I saw now robins in the Stafford Street alley. Last night, Rod said that all the leaves fell from his pear tree on Sunday the 27th.

2007: The late third quarter of the Sandhill Crane Moon brought sightings of sandhill cranes the village. Dorothy Smith wrote that "on Friday (11/30) about noon, I heard some strange honking noises and saw very high up in the sky, two small groups of big crane-like birds circling over my yard on N. Winter Street. I knew they must be sandhills because I'd just read about the Sandhill Crane Moon in your Almanac. Well, I grabbed my cell phone and called my friend Katie Egart over on Pleasant St. and she caught a glimpse of them as they formed into a V and headed due south. She called her friend Chris Glaser who was working over on Whiteman Street, and he saw them too. What a glorious and unexpected sight it was!"

2009: Finally, the weather turns wintry, the sky mottled in the sunset, cold violet and pale rose, the wind cutting through me when I go out to the back yard. In a few days, the first really hard freeze is due. Downtown, the pear trees have lost almost all their leaves.

2010: All-day rain moves across Ohio, tornadoes strike the South, deep cold and flurries in the North as a high-pressure system ends November.

2011: A tree full of dozens of buzzards at 8:30 this morning along the highway south to Xenia. Catherine called to say she had seen a flock of about 100 sandhill cranes flying south across the fields west of town.

2012: A mild night, full moon, only scattered clouds. A cardinal was singing when I went outside for firewood at 7:10 this morning, round moon in the west trees, sky blue green with dawn. Crows came by at 7:50. When I walked Bella before 9:00, a cardinal sang, and small flocks of starlings whistled in the high branches above me.

This afternoon, with a high in the middle 50s, the squirrels in the back trees were swinging back and forth, chattering and chattering. I mowed the lawn and mulched leaves for the last time, weeded the lily area near the trellis and covered the mower and the porch table for winter. A cardinal sang in mid afternoon, and the sparrows were chattering all the while in the bare forsythia. At sundown, the sky was orange and violet for more than half an hour.

2013: On the way back from Wisconsin, only one large flock of starlings, some filling all the high-tension wires across the freeway, others circling, landing, feeding. No large hawks seen.

2014: Walked with Bella in the mild morning, wind warm from the south. Robins were chirping all around, starlings whistling and clucking, a nuthatch called in the alley, and cardinals sang near Limestone Street and again near Dayton Street. In the far south garden, I found the first buds, lips smooth and flushed, on two hellebores in the hellebore patch. This is the earliest I've noticed them; they probably take shape slowly through November, hold on stubbornly through the winter.

2016: The last zinnia stalks piled against the north edge of the yard, the back garden area now close to ready to prepare for planting in the spring. The New England aster seeds thin quickly now. Quince and bamboo leaves cover the netting I have across the pond. Only the honeysuckles hold, and the Chinese elm keeps leaves, pale green and high. The pear trees by the post office are deep golden and shedding hard. Here in Yellow Springs, warmth and sun, then gentle rain in the evening. Throughout the South, deadly tornadoes and wildfires.

2017: The mild weather continues, and the koi rose to take their food this morning for the first time in several weeks. Now clouds and light rain, the slow approach of Early Winter. In my front hedge (but not in the woods), the honeysuckles are bare.

2018: In a few days of mild and foggy weather between cold fronts, Jill's autumn crocus came up, stalky and fragile, then fell over the next day. Down High Street, the cherry-size fruits are falling from a Bradford pear tree. In the north plot where I planted daffodils, an old poppy plant that I had turned under preparing the ground for bulbs has pushed up, a fragment of the past and of second spring.

2019: Mild and misty rain. A cardinal sings before dawn. The pond cover is ready to be removed, all the quince, English elm and late mulberry leaves down. My sidewalk is covered with the last of Lil's maple leaves. At the pond, the cypress trees are shedding more rapidly, maybe three-fourths down. Leslie reports white-throated sparrows throughout the period, and one "huge noisy flock of 600+ Grackles & Starlings in our treetops, yacking as they eat berries from Black Cherry and Hackberry trees; stayed approx 1/2 hour around 12 noon, then moved eastward on South College Street for awhile." Also one hermit thrush, many goldfinches. The month ends four degrees below average, rainfall about half of average, but three inches of snow fell.

2020: The first snow of the winter falling as the sky grows light. Three inches by later in the day and through the night. The average temperature for the month was 47.7 degrees, the highest I have recorded since 1980, just a tenth of a degree higher than 1985, almost ten degrees warmer than the chilly average of last November. And the news reports that this November was the warmest on record for the planet. At the end of the day, John called to report Doug had seen sandhill cranes flying over his farm north of Spring Valley, about twenty miles south of Yellow Springs.

2021: The average for this November: 41.8 degrees, about a degree or so below normal, precipitation: 2.79 inches, snowfall: 1.2 inches.

2022: The average temperature for this November: 45.4 degrees, a couple degrees above normal. Precipitation: rain 1.91 inches, snow 2.4 inches.

2023: Robins still calling in the morning. Monthly temperature average: 44.7. Rainfall: 1.56 inches. Snowfall only a trace.

Notes on the Annual Gathering of Crows
Near Yellow Springs, Ohio
(written for the Yellow Springs News)

Several miles northwest of Yellow Springs, Ohio, thousands of crows congregate every year to feed and fly restlessly back and forth among the corn and soybean fields. I've long wondered about their gathering that occurs regularly between the middle of November and the end of January. Now several notes in an old copy of *Science News* have given me new food for thought about this mysterious phenomenon.

The first article was a report on the tentative findings of Richard Potts, a Smithsonian archeologist, on brain evolution and climatic shifts. Potts contended that the human brain developed most rapidly in response to "frequent, jarring environmental shifts" - especially changes in climate. Making use of evidence from excavations in southern Kenya, Potts suggested that hominid toolmakers not only survived, but also actually grew bigger brains in response to their rapidly changing ecosystem. Other species, less inclined to adapt, and became extinct. This conclusion supports other studies that suggest Stone Age peoples may have advanced in an evolutionary sense precisely because of the on-going crises inherent in their rugged existence.

The research done by Potts dovetails with the second article from *Science News* - a report concerning ecologist Gavin R. Hunt's studies on *Corvus moneduloides*, the resourceful crows of the Pacific island of New Caledonia. Hunt discovered that these birds make tools out of sticks and leaves. In addition, he found that their tools showed "a high degree of standardization" and had hooks and barbs - features that are absent from the tools of chimpanzees and which only appeared in human evolution with the advent of *homo erectus*.

Potts and Hunt's theories may have special significance here in Yellow Springs. Given the magnitude of environmental events that have overtaken the Earth in the past century, I can surmise what it is our crows are doing on these cold autumn and winter days. If this epoch is, as many say, the most cataclysmic for the planet since the extinction of the dinosaurs, the crows may be convening to discuss survival. Already at the stage our hominid ancestors reached a few hundred thousand years ago, their brains are probably swelling from the cruel challenges of rapid climatic transformation, and they are doing science – observing, experimenting, sharing. They could be making tools.

While we, *Homo urbanus* and *Mulier urbana*, safe and warm in our climate-controlled habitats, are losing ground. Having learned at last to protect ourselves from the very forces that gave birth to our ingenious cerebrum, we need no longer fear the sun nor the snow nor the beasts; we have no hardships other than those we inflict upon ourselves; separate from nature, we devolve.

First thaw, early spring, breakup, middle spring, late spring, early summer, midsummer, high summer, late summer, early fall, Indian summer, first killing freeze, high fall, Late Fall, first snow, Early Winter, midwinter, high winter, late winter, first thaw, early spring breakup...more names than months, more names than days, more names because more names are needed.

Gary Paulsen, *Clabbered Dirt, Sweet Grass*

Bill Felker has been writing almanacs and nature columns for newspapers and magazines since 1984, and he has published the annual *Poor Will's Almanack* since 2003. His radio version of *Poor Will* is broadcast weekly on WYSO, a National Public Radio station, and it is available on podcast at **www.wyso.org.** His collections of essays, *Home is the Prime Meridian: Essays in Search of Time and Place and Spirit, Deep Time Is in the Garden*, and *The Virgin Point: Meditations in Nature*, along with the twelve volumes of *A Daybook for the Year in Yellow Springs* are available on Amazon.

For more information, visit Bill Felker's website at
www.poorwillsalmanack.com